CW00322140

"Whose Space Is It Anyway?"

an unofficial guide to the sites that changed **the world**

Published in 2007 by
INDEPENDENT MUSIC PRESS
Independent Music Press is an imprint of I.M. P. Publishing Limited
This Work is Copyright © I. M. P. Publishing Ltd 2007

"Whose Space Is It Anyway?"
An Unofficial Guide To The Sites That Changed The World
by Joe Shooman
All Illustrations by and © Alex Jackson 2007
Except Page 39 by Alfie Blue
All Rights Reserved

British Library Cataloguing-in-Publication Data.
A catalogue for this book is available from The British Library.
ISBN: 0-9552822-1-7 and 978-0-9552822-1-8

Cover Design by Fresh Lemon.
Edited by Martin Roach and Rachel Bean.
Manufactured in the EU by L.P.P.S. Ltd Wellingborough Northants NN8 3P

Independent Music Press
P.O. Box 69, Church Stretton, Shropshire SY6 6WZ
Visit us on the web at: www.impbooks.com
or at: www.myspace.com/independentmusicpress
and: www.myspace.com/whosespaceisitanywaybook
For a free catalogue, e-mail us at: info@impbooks.com
Fax: 01694 720049

"Whose Space Is It Anyway?"

an unofficial guide to the sites that changed **the world**

by Joe Shooman

Independent Music Press

marketing publisher author illustrations

Contents

Introduction

This book is already obsolete.

Honestly. Just look on the web.

Just look *at* the web. Things change so fast these days.

How can you ever seek to pin an inherently transient medium down to a fixed point in time and space? Like the definition of morality, the concept of justice and the game of rugby union, it is by nature a futile exercise best avoided.

Most of the stuff in here was out of date ages ago.

Conceptually, however, a large, chunk of the discussions presented herewith essentially predate the internet.

And, if you don't mind me saying so, you look lovely in those socks you have on today.

They match your eyes.

So we may as well crack on with it for now and see how it goes.

Whose Space Is It Anyway?

Joe Shooman

What's all this about space and why is it suddenly mine?

That there Interweb has changed: MySpace, Bebo, Friendster, Faceparty and others have brought a new concept of social networking to websites on the internet, within which anyone who has a computer can sign up, usually for free, to share thoughts, dreams, discover new music and write all manner of nonsense in their blog.

Any further questions?

What's a computer?

Eat y'self fitter.[1]

Er, yeah. What's an internet?

A vast network of networks of computers connected through a packet switching system and communicating through a series of standard, shared protocols. When you connect to the network – in other words, when you go online – you can talk instantly to anyone anywhere in the world, providing they are also connected to the network and you know where to find them. It's often known, inaccurately,[2] as the World Wide Web. It is, essentially, a place that stores shitloads of pornography.[3] It can be thought of as a big, massive, humungous, titillating encyclopaedia of perversion, except that there are no 'pages' to speak of as traditionally defined. All the information is on screen, thus you've suddenly got a big new telly where you can choose when and what you would like to watch, read or otherwise enjoy and endure. You will not be holding a book[4] in your hand. Which obviously leaves hands free for other purposes. Rumour has it that there is also other information available online. As yet, this is somewhat unproven.

So let me get this straight. I think I got the bit about porn; that sounds pretty cool. Where do the spiders come in? And why do they switch packets? Sounds depraved already.

Don't be stupid. But yeah. The depraved bit is fairly accurate.

Sheesh. Social networking?

Yeah, it's a bit like talking to loads of strangers you'd never actually want to meet in real life, except because each and every one of you is online from your own house, college or library[5] then you can pretend to be a thousand times more interesting, sexy and knowledgeable than you really are.[6] In the olden days people had to rely on *actually knowing each other* and found out things about each other by 'talking' with their mouths, rather than with their fingers. You should try it sometime.

You're just getting aggressive now.

Don't fuck with me, I'm a ninja.[7]

Gah. You're no use. I just wanted to learn about why I suddenly appear to own some space. I didn't pay for it, and I've no access to a rocket either.

Look, it's not space in a James Kirk sense, no matter how regular his bowels are these days cause of the cereals he eats. It's cyberspace. It doesn't really exist. It's like virtual reality, except about elvisly-twelvety thousand billion[8] times more shit than The Lawnmower Man would have you believe.

Cyberspace?

It's… okay, fair enough, let's rewind… this conversation is getting us nowhere. I think we'll have to go back in time to the 'book' configuration to sort this all out. Don't worry. It's got some nice, reassuring pictures in it, and later it has the word 'boffin' at regular intervals.

Part One:
Computers Get Small And The Web Gets Big

A Brief History Of Computers

In the olden days, computers were massive. Huge; humungous; of an enormous vastness unimaginable to modern eyes. They were so big, in fact, that to own one you'd need a whole floor of an office building spare. These old computers were so mind-meltingly big that *you could walk around inside them.*[9] They ran on spit, string, vacuum tubes and millions of megawatts of electricity, and sometimes they could process difficult sums so fast that you would only have to wait around eighteen hours to find the answer to a complex problem such as, "What do you get if you multiply six by nine?"[10] They were, as today's 'kids' would say, "OMG, like, totally mega-cool? They totally, like, pwn? LOLercopter".

In order to operate one, presuming you had several million quid – or whatever they used to use as cash[11] when the world was all, like, black and white and scratchy, and everyone walked around dead fast, dressed in bowler hats and penguin suits and looked like Charlie Chaplin[12] – you had to don a white coat and go almost entirely bald, and perched on your head would be a pair of black, Bakelite NHS glasses with lenses so thick you'd have to nick stained glass from the local church to replace them. And you'd definitely need a clipboard. You had to, basically, look like Denis Norden.

Over the years, computers got smaller, and cheaper, with chip technology[13] enabling exponential miniaturisation and therefore leading to mass-produced economies of scale, cultural ubiquity and the consequent increases in processing ability and power that go with an adopter curve in technological cultural terms, until eventually everyone had a computer on their laps.[14]

A Brief History Of The Internet

The Russians launched a satellite in 1957 which had a dog in it. The Americans were a bit put out by this, so their Advanced Research Projects Agency hooked up with another bunch of American boffins who'd previously glued together all the radar systems in the Land Of Plenty. The geezer in charge of ARPA's project – specifically working through and with the IPTO[15] – thought it'd be a wizard wheeze to glue all their computers together by phone leads so their scientists could share information about flying dogs and discuss how this new breed of airborne canine could lead to the prosecution of more Communists. His name was J.C.R. Licklider, which is a brilliant name and probably one of the more compelling reasons why he was picked for the job in the first place.

By 1969, the concept of a packet switching network had been implemented.[16]

A packet switching network works a little like this. You're in Toxteth, right, and you have in your possession a pair of rather natty fur-lined, zip-up slippers that you would quite like to send to your nan in Aberdeen, because it's her birthday and she has told you more than once that, oooh, isn't it terrible how the winters are getting so cold these days? So you pack up the slippers, taking care to sellotape your fingers together a few times, eventually master this fiendishly tricky conundrum, lose her address, phone your folks to find out the postcode, address your completed parcel, put far too many stamps on it because it's raining and you can't be bothered walking to the post office to weigh it properly, and finally whack this lovely gift in any postbox – and, through a series of magical events, eventually at the other end, the parcel of slippers will be taken by a hung-over postie to her door.

What happens in between goes something along the lines of this: a postman in Toxteth picks up the parcel, [17] and sends it via any of the post offices of the UK anywhere in between, taking *any route* between said post offices, before the Aberdeen postie picks it up at the other end to take to your nan, whose feet are now at roughly the temperature of the core of the sun because thirteen of her grandchildren have taken note of her multifarious and heavy hints over the last year. They've all bought her pairs of natty fur-lined, zip-up slippers from the same manufacturers for her birthday, so now she's wearing thirteen pairs at once so as not to offend anybody, and is consequently roughly nine foot tall. The post offices in the middle of this slipper-sending system are the nodes of the network. And as everyone knows, if you have no nodes you are not only in a lot of strife, but you also smell awful. [18]

This was the ARPANET, and it was generally held up as one of those rare American concepts that you could quite happily refer to as A Good Idea. So much so that by 1981, similar networks had sprung up to cover not just America, but Canada, the UK, Hong Kong and Australia. Subsequently, the internet as we know and don't understand it, was born on January 1, 1983, when the National Science Foundation sorted out a link between all the U.S. universities. So, during the Eighties loads of other networks came online and people started talking in pubs about 'An Internets' and how easy it was to talk to someone on the other side of the world about the latest developments in C5 technology instantly, without even having to get up from your ZX81 and use the telephone. Also in 1983, a young Matthew Broderick hacked into the NORAD system and almost started World War III,[19] which was only prevented by a swift game of Tic-Tac Toe.[20]

Of course, 'the internet' is a buzzy and in part meaningless term which basically describes a number of networks networked together, or not, as the case may be. It's only in retrospect that we can identify the various proprietary protocols as a somewhat chaotic, but nonetheless conceptually unified, whole – it is a Wide Area Network. So that's what we'll do: the principle of unifying the varying hardware and software systems to get them to speak to each other in a language that they all understand is what we're on about here.[21] If you want it to get more techy than that, you'll just have to talk to someone with a balder head than me, who wears big NHS glasses and a white coat, as discussed in the wiki 'A Brief History Of Computers' a couple of pages back.

And so grew a network of networks of computers glued together – eventually, on a worldwide basis[22] – down phone lines and able to access information hosted either on the computers themselves or on designated computers which act as servers for the information.

By the end of the Eighties, the internet was, like, all over the place. [23]

What People Did On An Internets In The Olden Days And How They Learnt How To Talk Badly On Purpose

It's all very well to go on about some brave new world of robo-flip full of cheeky computers communicating with each other, but the unavoidable fact is that behind each computer terminal is an operator. A *person*.

And if people like to do anything, they like to talk, and boy, m'boy, don't they like to talk. A lot.
They talked.

People posted questions and messages to each other through discussion groups, instant relay chat and message boards about the possibility that one day Rover may yet evolve into a soaring barker; they talked through electronic mail; they chattered and they cried; they told bad jokes and they blustered; they spammed and they spoke; they made dates and planned dastardly deeds; they shared tales of trust and truth.

They also developed a shorthand language of nonsense that is still in use today. Hacker Slang has been one of the driving forces in the continuing flux of English language. Any noun can be made into a verb, says English, more or less, largely because English is an idiotic mongrel language that makes very little rational etymological sense, and has random floating syntax rules seemingly invented by a team of blind-drunk Bonobos after a night on the absinth. Hacker Slang embraces this vague principle, and says that where possible a noun should be made into a verb.

"I have a MySpace: MySpace me."[24]

Communicating electronically means developing what you might call a digital identity; revealing things in text that you'd never dream of talking about in the farrago of tactile mess that is known as 'Real Life'. It wasn't all that different to our online lives now; it just looked a bit rubbish.

Playing Games With Strangers Naked In The Dark
Is always fun.

Why Playing Games With Strangers Naked In The Dark Is Always Fun
It is 1986. You own a Commodore 64. You subscribe to Quantum Link[25] and are connected to the Internet. Q-Link's online features include electronic mail;

participatory message boards, news, instant messaging and all manner of people-connection chatty-chatty tools.

You can speak to people without leaving your Commodore 64.

You don't have to turn the lights on.

You don't even have to get dressed.[26]

Q-Link also hosts games. One of these games is Lucasfilm's Habitat: a virtual, multi-user, graphically interfaced immersion environment in which your character – your avatar – can walk around the virtual world interacting with other avatars, questing, molesting and generally being interesting. You meet each other in this virtual world and talk to each other by entering text on your keyboard. And, because there are none of those restrictive, multi-choice parameters that beset the traditional model of adventure games, you can therefore say anything you like.

You can have a conversation. Humans like to talk.

Habitat therefore enables another level of communication within a virtual community that develops its own governmental and social rules dependent on the individual users and their real-world identities.

Habitat is a graphical, digital social networking tool.

A Brief History Of The World Wide Web
"The Web, when it originally was created, was a document management system."
> – Alexander Cameron, Digital TX Limited.

Whilst a generation dressed in legwarmers and deely boppers, grooved on down to the sound of Level 42 whilst watching Kids from *FAME* and simultaneously messing about with 2D simulations of real life on their

Commodore 64s,[27] rather serious and clever people were sat in dark cellars messing about with computer codes.

One of these clever bods was King Boffin, Tim Berners-Lee, who – to all intents and purposes – invented the World Wide Web.[28] We don't need to go into it much here, but suffice to say that after the usual daftness of trying, and failing, to convince people that the idea of developing *and standardising* a thing called hypertext, in order to index and cross-reference the body of information available on the internet, was intrinsically sound, he only went and wrote the blimmin' thing himself – an easy-to-use browser system that basically made some sense of the information previously online, and by its cunning nature therefore enabled every user to generate their own content to piggyback on the internet.[29]

By 1993, the rubbishly acronymed WWW was made available unilaterally as an open-source, non-proprietary protocol system, and designed as a read/write interface. Eventually, as long as you had access to the internet, somewhere to host your content, and the software to hand, you could put up your own web page – complete with graphics and all the bells and whistles you could possibly envisage, from nasty pink backgrounds to animated flying dogs. With hardware and memory costs going down as fast as processor and connection speeds were going up, the rise of the home computer as part of most Western households coupled with Berners-Lee's foresight ushered in what remains the biggest revolution in human communication and memetic consciousness since my last book was published.[30] Or the invention of crustless bread. Anyway, he's a Sir these days, so show him love.

What People Used The Web For In The Old Days

"The point of the internet, when people were first using it," says Daryl Bamonte, ex-Depeche Mode road manager and occasional member, and subsequently manager of The Cure, "when I became aware of it in '95, it was all supposed to be free. Then they didn't even want regulation, which was a bit of a Wild West ethic."

"I remember being on the phone to Feeder's manager," laughs David Rowell of Bigger Picture Media, "calling

him up from New York and saying, 'You'll never believe it – all these people have got these 'www' things!'"

Inevitably, the freedom engendered by the opening up of cyberspace to all and sundry was swiftly swooped upon by the commercial sector: one thing that you can be sure of in life is that where people congregate, so there will be hawkers, hustlers and subsequently a marketplace for anything and everything you can envisage. The early years of the web, the mid-to-late Nineties, were no exception. The money-lenders were firmly in the temple, and they weren't for movin', no sirree bucko.

People have been buying and selling goods since time immemorial; that this new congregation space happened to be a virtual online one was merely a new forum for financial transaction. The question, however – then, as now – was how to find the most elegant and cost-effective way to connect the customers with the things they're keen to buy. And, because the web-browsing experience, in contrast to a traditional store-based buying experience, doesn't require a physical location, online stores exploded and expanded very quickly; amazon.com led the way with an innovative technology add-on that allowed user reviews and matched the customer with other goods they might like based on their buying history.[31] The freedom to surf the web was the freedom to buy; the freedom to buy was the FREEDM to be; the data trail people left, however, was an entirely different matter.

Enter The Pop-Up

Annoying things. Advertising is the bane of any insane capitalist system. And soon there were programs launching new beeping, blasting, bloody annoying browser windows all over the place with one misplaced click. Y'know, like, sheesh guys, leave me alone you sods. *I'm trying to surf for ~~porn~~ the latest news.* Conversely, however, web advertising also monetises systems that otherwise would require user subscription and restrict access to parts of the web. In a sense, it's a necessary evil that allows a modicum of freedom. That's the theory, anyway. [32

Spam, Spam, Spam, Spam, Spam, Spam, Spam, Spam, Spam, Spam, Spam And Chips

Electronic mail – email – has sped up human communications considerably. It's so much part of our lives these days that there's a whole generation growing up into positions of power that has *never worked without it*. And as more and more people have come online, so they – we – started chucking out another verb: instead of handing out phone numbers after another resolutely unsuccessful date, ~~Joe Shooman is~~ people are fobbed off with a swift, 'Email me'.

The problem with this is that once your email address is flying around the net then anyone can access it. Before long, your pristine inbox (in which you'd lovingly arrange and rearrange these curious communications) is filled with advertisements for Viagra and lovely, thoughtful offers to Keep It Up All

Night! Erectile Dysfunction Click Here! Breast Enlargements Twenty Dollars!(33) More sinisterly, attachments appear in these emails which, on clicking, would infect your computer with all manner of nasty spy programs designed either to nick your bank details, take control of your computer remotely in order to turn it into a zombie host to send out yet more spam, or, just for the hell of it, bugger up the hard disk entirely. The scamps. Regardless of its intent, 'spam' has come to mean something entirely different than the stuff you see in the shops.(34)

These days, email is a necessary evil; for the moment. But we'll get to that later. In part thanks to the spammers and in part cause kids are basically an impatient bunch of monkeys, soon enough the concept of instant relay chat was dug up and instant messaging programs such as MSN Messenger, ~~Shooman Messengerô~~, Yahoo! Messenger and so on slid themselves into the communications tangle.

Another Sphere Is Born

One of the buzzwords of the next evolution of the web – 'Web 2.0' – which is pretty much what we're on about to be honest, is something known as 'citizen journalism'. The justification goes something like this: As everyone has access to the web, everyone can not only read the information up there, but also they can write anything they like about anything they like. This is meant, on paper, to indicate a levelling of the playing field and an ultimate democratisation of the media. No longer, goes the argument, will people have to rely on the traditional media outlets to present them information. No, no, no: now everybody can be a journalist, a commentator, a columnist and a writer. All you need is a weblog and the world will listen! [35]

Kinda. You sort of need to find people who are at all arsed about your random musings on boys you fancy, half-baked diaries of how your landlord has bought you a new fridge, and quarter-baked libels scattergunned at all and sundry. [36] There are more who shout than who listen; and so began an odd period where personal

diaries were chucked on the web willy-nilly for everyone to see. The blogosphere was born. Rejoicing followed.[37]

Some Of The Music Industry Starts To Think, "Hey Now, What's All This About?"

Out of chaos comes order (and cash, according to Malcolm McLaren); the growing noise of information on the web needed people to make sense of it. And, as ever, it was the more independent-minded amongst the music industry that led the way.

"I remember when Mute started up www.mute libtech.com,"[38] recalls Daryl Bamonte. "It was in '95, very ahead of the game – they had a little network that you could go on; there was a forum, and you could send messages to each other." Because, hey, people like to talk.

There was still a suspicion about the web from many quarters at this stage, not least from the traditional print media; the revolution had barely begun. Contrast this with the *New Musical Express*, whose current website editor Ben Perreau is thankful for the foresight of his predecessors.

"The *NME* site exists as the peek of the 55-year-old traditional *NME* into the digital world," says Perreau. "It started like that in 1996 because some clever people here decided that the internet was coming and they should do something about it. And if they didn't do anything about it then it was gonna come along and wash over them whether they liked it or not. So they created a music website to get things off the ground. Back then it was neon green and neon pink during that particular phase – some crazy, garish colour, using that age-old publishing technique of using fluoros and neons and bright colours to try and attract people's attention. It came very much from the publishing stable. To their credit, they were quite prescient I think with creating a music website, when only the MP3 and Napster were just kicking off, really."

The increasing affordability of home studio software such as Cubase, Pro Tools and Logic was also opening things up further; more music was being recorded, more cheaply than ever before. The difference this time was that there was also a way to fire it round the world very, very quickly; not only was home bandwidth getting faster and bigger, the song files themselves could be compressed to a lower quality – but much smaller, and still perceptually reasonably-acceptable – MP3[39] file, which led to firecrackers going off all over the place. Files were starting to be shared at a faster rate than ever before: as the Nineties drew toward their end, this worldwide equivalent of playground cassette-tape swapping reached epidemic proportions.

Napster And p2p Threatens To Destroy The World As We Know It

Peer To Peer software essentially, simplistically, bypasses the web client-server protocol, and connects computers directly over the net. This means that files can be transferred in the ol' hush-hush, without Mister Interweb ever knowing a deuce about it. It's a bit like meeting up with your nan in a transport café somewhere in between Toxteth and Aberdeen, and passing her a pair of furry slippers[40] in a brown bag under the table, for which she might exchange a packet of boiled sweets all fused together and covered in some unidentifiable fluff from God knows where.

It wasn't a new concept; Usenet users had been firing things at each other before the web had ever been invented and, of course, Home Taping had been Killing Music for many years before that (plus it had the coolest logo of any anti-piracy campaign ever, with that totally awesome tape 'n' crossbones thing goin' on). This new file swapping was most prominently, but not exclusively, taking place on Napster, an MP3 file-sharing program invented, coded and implemented by Shawn Fanning in 1999 and quickly jumped upon by people naughtily sharing copyright material. The concept of music being freely available appealed greatly to the new generation; not so the major labels, who could see revenue streams crumbling away before their eyes. Most famously, big hitters including Lars Ulrich of Metallica, Dr. Dre and Madonna flipped out about it, and Napster subsequently went into bankruptcy.[41] Lawsuits against music users began to kick in, but the genie had been let out of the bottle.[42] The inevitable consequence of Napster's demise was that a whole host of new file-sharing programs (whose users, more often than not, were continuing the compelling practice of swapping all manner of material in which they did not hold copyright) were sucked into the vacuum left by that particular piece of software. The labels who'd released the music weren't gettin' no cash, dude, and neither were the musicians getting their recoupable-advanced, tour-supportless, packaging-deductioned dirty copper coin micro-percentages as a result. Bad news all round: but, hey, this is the web, remember. The Wild West. And everyone wanted monetary control of it.

How The Bubble Burst, With Splendid Consequences

In short, this is how the latter years of the Nineties went: Millions of users of the web = millions of users with cash = millions of pounds being spent by venture capitalists and stock market speculators on half-baked web 'businesses' that would never return on their money = millions of dogs bought = big stock market crash.

That's basically it.

This is important because the bursting of the dot.com bubble in 2000–2001 filtered out a lot of the sharks and shysters who were shouldering each other out of the way in a desperate scramble to try and monopolise the marketplace. Not the first time this has happened in the Western world, and certainly not the last time, either. It's called Capitalism.

The real power, of course, lies in the users; not quite 'the hope lies in the proles', but nevertheless the message writ strong was this: People don't like to be sold *at*, but they do still want to be sold *to*.

Another Verb Is Born

"I remember, in the early days of the internet, being astonished at AltaVista," says Conor McNicholas, editor of weekly new music bible, *NME*, "AltaVista could effectively do a word search on the internet – it was the most amazing thing! And then somebody showed me Google, and you just never go back."

Making sense of the massive amount of information

on the web was taken another logical step further by one of the few companies to have actually based their dot.com activities on both sound and unconventional business ideas, and therefore not only survive, but blastin' well thrive. Google's innovative Page Ranking system[43] made them the most elegant search engine out there; it also – eventually – raised rather significant amounts of cash by selling advertising space targeted to and by the search through their AdWords technology. A net project that had literally begun in the garage of a student had become the last word on web search, and a major player in this whole kaboodle. AdWords was also a boon for those rare bloggers whose readership was registering high traffic, and people actually make cash this way these days. Mad, isn't it.

"If you need to find it," says this weird English language we appear to have developed, "Google it."

Poor old Jeeves, nobody asks him anything anymore.

Hello Mister Precedent

The web had come of age, of sorts; a new digital communication had firmly planted itself in the work and personal lives of a generation. Emails, instant messages, powerful search engines for images, text and a growing number of online music, entertainment and educational sites; as the Millennium bugs started crawling about, the digital world was buzzing and alive.

And So End The Viagra Years

There's nothing to read here really, it's just how the ever-affable Daryl Bamonte refers to the first few years of the web and I thought it was a good way to sum it up before we get onto Part Two.

I'll give you a moment to relish the pun. See you after this blank page.

Part Two
Social Networking Sites

The fact that everyone was pretty much on the web by the mid-to-late Nineties was one thing; how to contact them was a much more difficult proposition. Sure, you know their names, but which IP are they using? Which server? Which client? More specifically, how do you find that lass who first induced priapic glee in the ol' fuzzy downbelows behind the bike sheds?

A new breed of websites began to emerge, sites that would seek to wrap up and re-centralise communications from the wide-eyed and confusing mess that the web had become. And the new buzz became 'social networking'.

"It's all about social networking," agrees David Rowell, such is the genius of the preceding paragraph, "In effect it's just mirroring the moves that were made five years previously, when you track people down through your band's website, then you'd go straight to the forum to have a chat. Not necessarily to talk about the band; to talk about what you're having for tea. You think 'blog' – well, actually, it's just a conversation."

Sites would try, with varying degrees of success, to pull together all the new conversational communications possibilities in one easy package, riding new browsers on the back of the fragmented and confusing mess that the web had become. Offering some or all of the capabilities of internal emails, instant messaging, profile and picture hosting, message boards, groups, classified ads, jobs, music, video and blogging, the new wave of the web was based on proprietary sites with their own individual design and demographic focus. However, this time rather than the information being hosted on servers far and wide – if not the client computers themselves – the digital identity storage was brought into a central server system, the interface of which everybody could understand as it was generally a simple and accessible, fixed design rather than the individually-built, and often confusing, bespoke websites that spidered and sprung the *fin de siecle* web. Networks within networks, webs within webs and communities within communities.[44] This move away from home hard drive storage of individuals' personal information, more than anything else, is an indicator of the attitude shift on which the still-vague and rather disingenuous term 'Web 2.0' is perhaps, in part at least, based. But more of that later. As the new millennium began to gain momentum, several of these newly focused sites began to struggle for prime position at the forefront of the new net wave.

How To Get In Touch With Everyone You Hated In School

"I was into CD-Roms in the mid-Nineties," says In The City founder, ex-Factory Records chief, current F4 Records boss and man of so many hats his head must be *massive*, the eminently quotable Anthony H. Wilson. "And my great friend Mark Geiger said, 'Fine, you're into

CD-Roms, Tony, I'm into the internet, let me tell you all the great developments in human culture and human technology are led by sex. And when was the last time that you saw a sexy CD-Rom?'"

For most people in the UK, the answer to the contact-finding conundrum was presented in May 2000 with the launch of Friends Reunited, set up by Steve Pankhurst in his back bedroom whilst pregnant wife Julie kept moidering on[(45)] about what her old friends might be up to. Free to sign up to, Friends Reunited is essentially a central database where the users can register which school and colleges they went to, set up a personal profile of current interests, upload pictures and search for other people who'd done the same. Its consequent user-generated personal profile content of one-upmanship and voyeurism reflect both the growing cult of digital identity-building, and, by association, historically wider human traits. It is addictive, indeed.

"It was probably one of the first examples where the internet did something that would have been completely impossible otherwise," says Jon Clark, responsible for marketing and product development at Friends Reunited. "It made something which would have been a right hassle – being able to locate friends – very, very easy. Another good example is the Genes Reunited website, which does the same for family history, which previously was very laborious, time-consuming and difficult to do; it democratises it and makes it very easy."

Friends Reunited is very much a social networking site based (loosely) round previous schoolin' 'n' stuff, and it remains widely popular, despite the fact that there's a (negligible, but nevertheless extant) yearly charge to send and receive unlimited emails therein. Its success was such that the site's membership snowballed from a seriously respectable three thousand guys 'n' gals in its first year to a current userbase of over fifteen million.

Such was the success of this old-friend-finding that babies have been plopping out all over the shop thanks to the website initially facilitating the contact that led to bringing lusty ol' flames back together – the first FR sproglet duly arrived in 2002. Conversely, such is the success of the site that people have been rather unguarded about some of the liaisons they've set up through it: during 2004 the papers went crazy-nuts, offering Friends Reunited as a possible causal factor in the rising divorce rate.[46] Of course, it wasn't; enabling technologies are always blamed for this sort of thing, be it home videotaping and subsequent distribution of ~~porn~~ copyright-controlled content or naughties using p2p software to send each other ~~porn~~ pre-release rough mixes of new Radiohead tracks.

After all, as Geiger explained to the redoubtable Mr. Wilson,[47] it's all about sex – and if people were using the site to make the two minutes of squelching noises happen, it's hardly the responsibility of the service itself, now is it? Bit harsh that. These are *people* talking to each other, remember?

Regardless of all that gubbins, Friends Reunited remains a strong player in its niche; the brand was bought by ITV in 2005 and offers a range of services having branched out into jobs, dating, genealogy and a series of nostalgia-music CD releases.

It fulfils a very specific core role, and does it well – but, arguably, it's just not perceived as being as *cool* as some of the other ones out there, with an older demographic not as interested in the bells and whistles evident on other sites. And it sure as hell ain't the killer web application that's permeated every part of a generation's social lives either.

This Website Is, Like, Way Cool. TOTALLY

Faceparty might just well be, though. The site was established way back in 1997 under the mightily fine and equally mightily ridiculous name of Captain Miracle by one Dave Bamforth, who had been a legendary underground party promoter with the spiky freedom of mind that had seen him emerge more or less unscathed from the rave scene of the late eighties.

Rebranding the site as Faceparty in 2000, Bamforth's intent was to provide, "a way to meet people from raves online, if you like. It kinda grew accidentally into something completely different but very successful."

A meeting place, then, for compatible alternative types, but Faceparty's focus lies in deeper waters; legendary parties organised by Bamforth and Faceparty provided a unique real-world focus to the site's capabilities, which were incisive and visionary for the era. They addressed the problems that the web itself had presented in contacting and possibly collaborating along with other individuals who have the same song dancing in their souls. More of that concept later; it's a very important one.

"We're the first community to tie chat, profiles and messaging together," continues the mohawked-up site founder. "There were chat sites before then, and websites where you could upload your photos before then, but there was never anywhere that tied it all together. It was just such a phenomenal success – without any marketing we got to seven million members. We've tried very hard to keep it underground, because as soon as parents find out about something it's very uncool. We'd have things like *Trisha* phoning up to get our old agony aunt, Grim Rita, on her show, and we'd be like, 'No! We don't want grannies watching *Trisha* knowing about us, we're trying to keep underground.' And that was kind of the secret of our success."

"It's ironic really, because in the dot.com boom I was between dodgy deals and manky rave businesses at the time," laughs Bamforth. "I needed a bit of cash just to start up some projects so I was consulting for web companies. They were all big dot.com start-ups, and they were all getting hundreds of millions ploughed into these ideas which were just stupid and would never work. I was trying to tout for investment to get Faceparty off the ground, in the Captain Miracle days, and no-one would touch it because they didn't believe it could be so successful. We exceeded our first year expectations in the first couple of months, so we beat what we predicted, and we turned profit within four months – which is unbelievable for any business. Not that it's just about money, but obviously it costs millions to run servers of this size. I'm glad we didn't get the investment in the dot.com thing because it wouldn't have worked. The levels of investment being given around were more than any kind of web business would ever make."

So the model could work; it is, largely, about credibility as much as it is about functionality. Log into Faceparty and you walk into an open-armed world where, no matter what your background or predilection, you can hook up with people just like yourself. The rave – punk – attitude, it seems, is alive and well. And *that* is a cause for rejoicing.

"It is what community is; like-minded people," Bamforth smiles. "It's not about 'Look at me'; it's about 'Look at you'. A lot of the other sites you see are very much, 'Look at me, look at my amazing profile, look at how amazing I am', but it's not about that.

It's about being part of something, not being the most important person in something. I think a lot of the competitors are based on 'who's better than the other' and I think they're missing the point, because that's not community. Community's about each other and 'team' rather than 'me'. What's that cheesy expression? 'There's no 'I' in Team!'"

"A good example might be, say, some gay guy in the closet at school where he's getting really bullied," concludes Bamforth. "On Faceparty he can go and meet other gay people, so if he's feeling alone and going to top himself cause he's 'the only gay person in the world' this opens the world up a little for him."

Faceparty's advanced features at the time of writing – the 'Cool Tools' that bring a more precise control over the communications abilities and general feel of the site for the individual user – require a level of subscription, but in the main, the site is free and its main features have become the blueprint for many other social networking sites bandied around in the press.

Friendster

Cast your mind back two or three years – a lifetime in web terms – and Friendster was *the* place to be. Everyone was on there. *Everyone*. Friendster, on its web launch in 2003, seemed to offer it all; personal profiles, messaging, connections between people that blossom and strengthen the inherent concept behind a social networking website – the most innovative being the ability to leave testimonials on the profiles of other users. Very quickly, people rushed en masse to get themselves on there, spending hour upon hour poring over lists of privately connected users, messaging each other, and generally slacking off from the work in front of them that day. It could have been the killer site.

Friendster should have taken over the world.

But it has not.

(Yet.)

Much like Friends Reunited, the idea behind Friendster's genesis lay in a particularly human experience. Founder Jonathan Abrams was a programmer in Silicon Valley, working on various applications, including Netscape – kinda the forerunner, in a typically complex net-type pathway, to the open source Firefox browser. The story, which is probably apocryphal, and certainly categorically denied by Abrams himself, runs something like this: frustrated at the lack of opportunities for himself and his busy-bee friends to hook up with potential dates, someone with the technical nous sets up a website that would make online communication easier and would swiftly build up a network to make new connections.[48]

The initial uptake was massive; by the autumn of 2003 Friendster had three million users. The media interest was commensurate with this success; people were even selling access to networks of musicians and 'cool community links' on auction site, eBay.[49] A version of contemporary commerce had crept, possibly for the

first time, into the strange realms of real-life transactions based on purely digital social networking content.

Crucially, perhaps, users could connect with each other only through direct friend links – rather than the open-to-search functionality of other sites that have since sprinted past Friendster. Friendster's crack-down on, and deletion of, fake profiles ('Fakesters') – those of celebrities, pets, household implements – helped further deflate the nascent energetic sign-up that had thrust the project to the forefront of social networking sites.

Crucially, also, Abrams admirably turned down a multi-million dollar offer from Google[50] to buy into Friendster, preferring to bring in independent investment and keep internal control of proceedings. Expansion into different territories and the planned addition of greater functionality promised a bright future; why should they need to cede control?

It was indeed an admirable, but fundamentally problematic, strategy. In shooting for the twin twinkling stars of expansion and explosion, somewhere down the line the technical side was overlooked: the site was notoriously beset by server downtime and overload, and appeared to some to struggle to cope effectively with the explosion of concurrent active logged-in users; profiles at that stage weren't customisable; and finally, the rebuffed Google put their investment into their own affiliated social networking site, Orkut.

(The story, however, may not be over: Friendster may yet hold a powerful trump card in all this gubbins... but first things first. Remind me about it later and we'll chat.)

A mass user-migration began, disillusioned ex-Friendsters reuniting in a gold-rush to one particular site which, *more than any other*, has become the avatar for the next phase of web communications. It has impacted not only on online socialising, but is forcing changes in attitude and altering working practices within the music and entertainments industries.

I think you kinda know where we're going next, so the rest of this page is blank to give us both some thinking time; in a minute we'll see if we both come to the same conclusion as to which site we're on about.

Part Three:
Space, The Final Front
~~Bottom~~ Ear

Well done.[51]

MySpace

"I'm a sucker for the internet. I was on Friendster when I noticed that a few friends had posted messages about what they had called 'The New Friendster', with links to MySpace. I hadn't heard of it and at the time I didn't really see the point of Friendster because I usually emailed, phoned or lived with the people I wanted to see. At the time MySpace was very new and as such I was among the first wave to join but it took about nine months before I started using it regularly. I had already stopped using Friendster ..."

– Raziq Rauf, Music Journalist

"It has the ability to do good but essentially is one big mess of various ideas tacked onto one fairly good idea of taking email and personal webspace to another level."

– Sean Adams, Drowned In Sound

There is much anecdotal debate over the precise history of MySpace;[52] one of the symptoms of the insanely fast turnover of the web – plus its constant revisionism – is often a lack of reliable archiving of news content.

Any web search for 'MySpace history' will return some intriguing, if unverifiable, spins and counter-spins on the past history of the site, its founders and their previous companies.[53]

The conclusions you may or may not draw from your surfing are entirely up to you. And what we will firmly state at this point is to take care in your inferences; the web is notorious for its access to dodgy data.

But let's stick to the facts here; if you want half-truths, says Aesop, ask the wily fox.

What is not in doubt, however, is the fact that since its 2003 launch, MySpace has exploded into the daily lives of a generation in a way that Friendster threatened to do but never quite managed. MySpace currently boasts the most accounts of any social networking site active on the internet; at the time of writing numbers exceed 120 million. Note that this is the *number of registered accounts*[54] – figures for the amount of *active users* are more debatable, although of course you could apply that logic to any of the sites discussed in this book. Internet analysts Comscore, however, registered the amount of unique visitors to MySpace during May 2006 as 51.4 million.[55] Whichever way you look at it, that's one heck of a lot of interested people; the data for the amount of active accounts in some ways is secondary to the killer fact that you don't need to be logged into the system – or even signed up to MySpace – in order to browse through its pages via any of the search engines currently available. This is one of MySpace's greatest and most compelling features – its stickability and reference abilities offsite.

Sammy Andrews, the UK's leading digital/viral consultant, was a very early user of the site. "It was really small," she muses. "There weren't all the mad designs of the pages, or adverts and the rest of it. Some of the MySpace designs now are so garish that it hurts my eyes to look at them! It was very much a social site; when I first saw it I thought it just looked like Faceparty. It didn't have the videos feature; the song player wasn't very reliable. The initial thing for me was to use it to keep in contact with someone in America; we could speak every day and see when each other was online."

"It built from there really. Watching it change ... they're updating it all the time, nearly on a daily basis. It did go from this social community site where it was purely user-driven – people speaking to each other – to a massive advert. But people jumped on the back of being able to update it and do things with it."

"Friends were getting in touch with me, people I hadn't seen for years; there was Friends Reunited where most people I know had gone and registered, but it was a pain in the arse – you couldn't get in touch with anyone unless you paid. MySpace, straight away, had a schoolfriend finder. MySpace took the best aspects of a lot of sites that existed and offered them all in one package."

"What they've gone off the back of," agrees IPTV guru Alex Cameron, "is all these different dating community sites whose business model is charging for messaging. By contrast, everyone you know's on MySpace they've got the critical mass issue and of course you don't have to pay to message people. You can do exactly what you can on all the other dating sites but all completely for free. Which is hilarious."

Very funny.

Ahem.

More of that later.

What MySpace Is

"There's two ways to look at MySpace," according to Ben Perreau of *NME*.com. "One is as an interesting social network, and maybe it's the future, and maybe it's a way to get everyone online, and it's kind of the product of the internet, if you like. The other way to look at MySpace, from my point of view, is that it's a slightly transitionary thing. We've now got to this stage where you can build all these tools into it, and websites are still a little bit too complicated for everyone to be bothered to make – though not everyone can be arsed to sit there and make a MySpace page either! But not everyone can be arsed to sit there and create a website from scratch. But, sooner or later – and Google are already doing it with Google pages – these kind of things are happening and I think MySpace is the early part of the curve where everyone's social identity moves into a digital realm, where everyone can communicate with each other on every platform. So in the same way that games consoles are creating digital identities for people, MySpace is the first place that genuinely created a digital identity for people in a more consummate fashion – better than Friendster, which didn't quite round off the edges enough for people to feel like there was actually some heart in it."

MySpace certainly offered more user-interactivity than ever before; the proliferation of 'Pimp My MySpace'-type sites on the web is testament to that. Whilst in the early days of the web, the visionary boffins envisaged everyone being able to design and publish their own pages, the reality was that even HTML was fiddly and too much like a new language for anyone who didn't look like Denis Norden to actually be able to absorb and implement. After ten years of being peddled and infected by Viagra spam, allied to the subsumation of digital life into day-to-day existence, however, a new generation is growing up more computer- web- and technology-savvy than ever. MySpace appears to present its users with a smorgasbord of hangaroundability:[56] from bulletins to send round your friends to instant messaging, powerful searches and forums, comedy, books and music, embedded video and audio content and that ever-compelling customisable profile. The site has very nearly become what you might think of as a gateway web browser – a self-contained microcosm of all that the kids would want on the web. It is, as *Daily Star* music journalist Joe Mott puts it, 'the internet made easy,' as well as a tool that, in the words of Faceparty's Dave Bamforth, shouts, 'Look At Me!'

"It's like a singles column for hipsters, i.e. middle to upper-middle class arty people with ambitions on being involved in media and arts in some way," offers Andy Capper, editor of the monthly magazine *Vice UK*. "People like that don't get jobs or opportunities in a conventional fashion. They network through friends and parties and by pretending to like terrible bands and artists. It's a powerful self-promotional device. A lot of these people are really self-obsessed [who isn't?] so having a tool to tell the world all about their personal foibles is an attractive prospect. It also gives shy people a way to talk to the opposite sex. There's rumours of MySpace orgies and stuff but the closest I've come to participating in one of these was unorganised and terrible and didn't really happen."

"So many of my friends spy on their ex-boyfriends and girlfriends on MySpace," laughs Lucy Hughes of loserkids.com, one of the new breed of online stores and social networks. "Such a high percentage of the usage must be either people spying on their exes or checking out potential guys or girls that they fancy."

"MySpace breaks down 'elite' barriers," purrs Radio One DJ, Huw Stephens. "Everyone's equal on there. You can get little cliques by going to Top 8s or whatever, the list of Top Friends, but it breaks down personal barriers and it can be revealing about personal lives. You can find out whether somebody wants to be in a relationship or not have kids, what star sign they are. You can find out about their sex lives – and see photos if you want to! But also, at the same time, it's a bigger picture with people putting exclusive movie clips on there and big artists like Billy Bragg putting new songs on there. It's like a big village hall back in the olden days, when people used to swap things with each other."

Intriguing…

How People Make The Sex On These Kind Of Sites

"MySpace is a global popularity contest. Although plenty of people don't use it like that, you'll find the photos still sort of creep in that direction. The type of people with no photos of themselves or just of other people or of completely irrelevant objects are the ones who obviously think they're TOO COOL for that. These are like the leather jacket-wearing metal-head types from a High School Movie in the early nineties. They probably smoke. Then there's the 'few to average' group who just have a few photos of themselves having fun with friends and stuff. This is mostly just because you can put them up and people can recognise you, and it's better to see you having fun than, say, murdering a tramp. Hence a lot of them involve drunken arseholes. Obviously, people only put ones of themselves looking remotely attractive on there. Human nature. After this, you just enter the realms of the ridiculous. There's people with five pages of photos on there now, all taken of themselves looking like complete nonces. There's kids who post bulletins about their

I Love my bed!

new photos and stuff, the ones who write stupid little messages on them or under them and all that. Then there's that face they all pull, lips to one side, hair all in the face. I think it's supposed to be some new variation on what 'cute' looks like but is closer to looking like a 'spaz'. Basically then, the photos are normally just a harmless bit of fun, but there's shitloads of dickheads using it to try and make themselves look attractive. Unsuccessfully."

– Geoff, Who Used To Be In A Band
But Isn't Anymore.

Not surprisingly, all the people in this bit here would only share their experiences if they could do it under false names. But, hand on heart, I promise that none of them are me, which I'm a little bit upset about to be honest. Anyways, the instant messaging and incognito searchability of profiles that MySpace offers has led directly to some serious shagging in real life.[57]

"My friend who's in a band told me about it," says Boypolar with a glint in his eye. "I signed up to look at her band's page but then didn't use the site for any other purpose for quite a while. But as soon as I put my photo up, I started getting messages."

"I did not expect to pull the first people I'd met in the real world from there to begin with, because I think most people on there are not using MySpace for that. Then people started adding me on my MSN and chatting with me; I started meeting up with guys who were not out (of the closet) and were up for no-strings encounters. I went about it in a methodical way with the gay boys to begin with. I searched for them, under the parameters of gay men between 25 and 35. This led to four brief encounters. One interesting thing about them all is that they haven't added me as a friend, nor I them. Our messages were always between ourselves."

"There was the one time this girl contacted me on MySpace to say hello," offers Bob De★★★★e.[58] "I'd never met her before, she was just browsing and liked my picture. Anyway, we went out a few nights later in Camden and I ended up bringing her back to mine, and that. It was good. But really the big story is with this girl in LA. Not long after I joined MySpace I had a look on Tom [Anderson, founder of ...] MySpace's page and this girl had left an amusing comment on his page.

I took a look at her profile and messaged her cause she seemed funny. We got talking, and carried on like this for a year until we ended up speaking on the phone a few times. Eventually she came over to

London for a trip with her friend. We snogged quite a bit, but nothing more, as she had a boyfriend. She went back home and finished with her boyfriend. So we're meeting up in New York in a few weeks to sort of close the deal. I'm thinking about moving to LA for a while to be with her, and see if it could work out. It's funny to think that none of this would have happened if I'd clicked on Tom's profile just a few seconds later, as that's how quickly new comments come through."

It's not a magic bullet to the old in-out, however.

"Like normal dating, it doesn't always go according to plan," Bob muses. "I've been out with a few girls I've met on there and it's not really gone anywhere after that. You can't just skip right to the shagging – you still have to dazzle them with your personality in person, without the cool front that MySpace provides."

Now, you'd think that one section of the community that has no need for such aids is those odd people known as 'students', what with their yard-of-alcopop, skool-disko, orgiastic, one-hour-of-work-a-week lifestyles. But, of course, they'll use any excuse, as someone whose name is definitely not Eddy Z★★★★l [(59)] explains.

"Tuesday used to be my day off of college! There is only one thing to do when you have days off college and a free house! GASH!!" he shouts rather breathlessly in my ear, all rubbery lips and flob, a bit like that chef off of the telly, [(60)] "I used MySpace as a sort of catalogue: have a browse on my friends list and then invite them

round. It was mostly a successful plan but sometimes it just didn't work! I recommend GASH DAY to any male on MySpace. It didn't just happen out of the blue, though. You have to put in some groundwork with the girls. I used the charm and cheek technique. They lapped up the charm and they love a bit of cheekiness."

And this is the next generation in power. Lord help us all.

Ask anyone who's on the site; they'll all have a tale of 'how their friends are always pulling on there.' [61] Enter scalpel-sharp thinker and indie label boss John Brainlove, who's dead sensible and clever and stuff and, entirely in character, gets straight to the crux of this odd business.

"Instead of asking for each other's numbers at the

end of the night, people ask for each other's MySpaces! And then they just study each other's MySpaces!" he offers incredulously. "Seeing who they're friends with, and what they've been saying to everyone – it's kinda like a little glimpse into someone's life. You can get such a good idea of someone just through communicating through words and text and chat: you can feel like you really, really know someone. I do wonder, if you meet someone first through MySpace, MSN and chatting loads in text, do you get a better idea of what they're like because the social pressure of chatting for hours has gone? You don't have the social awkwardness, or that sort of thing. You can just get on with chatting forever. It's as natural a way of meeting people as any. In fact, it's a lot less random than meeting someone in a bar or whatever, cause at least you can get quite an idea about them by looking at the comments they've left their friends, and what they're into. Like screening or something."

"I think it is happening to a lot to people that they feel more comfortable breaking the ice online than in the pub," agrees Boypolar. "I don't like people's profiles where you have to scroll down all the way through just to get to the basics. I want to know whether you're single, which team you bat for and how much you earn, not what your favourite colour is."

"A friend of mine met an American guy on MySpace," smiles Brainlove. "She was messaging him constantly and stuff, then she went to visit him and stayed over there for a few weeks. I looked on her profile the other day, and it says 'married'. She went over there, and they got married while she was out there. Now she's moving over to America!"

Good to end this bit on a nice note, cause I'm afraid to say that it all gets a bit darker for a while here, sorry. Don't worry, the Arctic Monkeys and loads of cool music types appear in twenty five pages or so. Plus a Playboy model, so y'know. Karma and all that.

And How These People Pay For It

Although revealing shedloads of personal information via your online digital identity can lead to all manner of late-night naughtiness, the fact remains that once you put something up there that's perhaps somewhat

indiscreet, everyone can see it – all they need to do is search for your MySpace profile.

"It's really unadvisable," Andy Capper says. "It's a device used by people to tell if their partners or spouses are cheating on them. Somebody tried to use it on me recently and it backfired spectacularly for them."

"Friends Reunited is slightly different," adds that site's Jon Clark, "because we like to have this walled garden which enables us to give people the protection and maintain the trust. When you send messages through the site it's done through the internal site mailbox so your personal email address isn't revealed. We deliberately don't release the content to search engines so if you searched my name you wouldn't find my Friends Reunited profile: that gives a lot of people a lot of confidence and reassurance that they can publish content and it won't be found by inappropriate people; the good thing is that you need to register to see anything, you need to find people at their school, then the right year. So there are several layers of formal or informal filters that mean pretty much that the people who are looking at what you've written are going to be people you don't mind seeing it. Even if it's just a sentence about the fact you're living in north London and you've got a couple of kids: you don't really want it out there."

"The internet's made publishing your thoughts super accessible," says Paul Rafferty of the splendid band, Hot Club de Paris. "Journals are no longer personal artefacts.

There is the option to publish them, so why not? It doesn't mean people actually read them."

There are even companies dedicated to screening, through sites such as Friendster and MySpace, profiles for salacious, unwise or incriminating evidence;[62] this has been famously used by employers, parents, police, schools[63] and partners alike – the clear message is, of course, rather obvious: don't put anything online that you don't want people to find out about. Because they blimmin' well goldurn *will* find it out. One of the most famous online spats of late is the messy brawl between Travis Barker and now ex-wife, Shanna Moakler: she threw a divorce party, to which he responded in a MySpace blog. The story whizzed round the world in minutes. Even worse, there have been reports of jilted wives searching for their exes' new flames, to the point of one who stands accused of hiring undercover rozzers posing as heavies and handing over cash to them in order to wipe out the new girlfriend.[64]

More sinisterly, the data trail has serious repercussions: unless you set your profile to private, you're in danger of not being considered for job opportunities; such is the growing trend of employers to take advantage of the open access to often deeply personal information.[65] In short, when you create your profile and are in the process of writing up your ~~social networking book~~ blog you may well be sat, naked, in the dark, smoking Camberwell Carrots in front of your personal computer – but every word you write and subsequently publish for all to see is a potential black mark against your name.

Morality on the net is as much built on shifting sands as the concept of honesty.[66] People like to talk. To you, but also *about* you. In the digital world, everything is at risk of becoming public domain, whether that be copyright content such as music or your own sexual adventures: the net does not discriminate. To Mister Interweb it's all just a series of zeroes and ones and this kinda thing just comes with the territory, buckeroo. Freedom ain't all shiny stones and setting up rumpy pumpy; FREEDM is not down to interpretation. The revolution will not be digitized.[67]

Danger! Danger!

"People see it as throwaway because they post these bulletins and they know who is getting them. If they don't trust those people they would either delete them from their friends list or not post the bulletin. They really do show a person's character because sometimes if there is a theme that repeats you COULD bring it up or avoid it in conversation in real life next time you see them because you can decipher from the bulletin exactly how sensitive they are with the issue. If, for instance, a lady keeps on mentioning in her bulletin that she's thirty years old and how she imagined her life would be different, you wouldn't make jokes about that with her. It's weird."

– Raziq Rauf, Music Journalist

Without labouring the point in a book that's supposed

bob emily marie family

to be on the lighter side of life, the fact that the web is supposedly open to everyone means that everyone is entitled to use it in any way they see fit. Geographical boundaries and different laws in different countries make the web a grey area at the best of times. The web exists in every country, but is bound to none.

MySpace itself, as social software, has based a lot of its success on the fact that sign-up is easy and free. It's aimed at those of fourteen and over, with profiles of its users who are under sixteen automatically set to private. All very admirable, but head over to the 'personal information' section and – whammo. You can change your date of birth to anything you choose. Whilst this in itself is another layer of interaction, it also means that on the site it's possible that people are not quite what they seem.[68] None of which is MySpace's fault.

Newspapers such as *The Daily Mail* have highlighted

and cited cases of paedophiles trawling the site to groom victims, one reporter posing as a fifteen-year-old girl and quickly garnering unwelcome attention online.[69] And although the media is prone to knee-jerk reactionary reporting, satirised famously and most notoriously by Chris Morris in 2001 in an episode of the provocative Channel 4 show, *Brass Eye*,[70] the fact that you can never be quite sure if people's digital identities are accurate or even honest is one of the conceptual quandaries of our age.[71]

In truth, fundamentally this is not a MySpace-created phenomenon by any definition; it is certainly not their fault; neither can it be put down to any of the social networking sites, the web itself or any kind of technology extant or yet to be invented. The facts are that MySpace themselves have held many meetings with concerned parents in order to discuss this problem, which is nothing to do with enabling technologies, and everything to do with the darker and more distressing facets of personal human morality. And that is a problem that has beset the world since the first days of social interaction.[72]

Part Four:

Professionalising And Monetising All This Stuff We're On About

"The time the 14–25-year-old spends turning the pages of magazines has massively reduced over the last ten years compared to the time they spend clicking a mouse. Whereas people my age would sit in their bedrooms listening to music and reading magazines, we're now online. And it's even worse for the younger people, so consequently you have to be in that space in order to get your messages across, and secondly you've got to utilise that space in order to create an experience offline. It's not

enough anymore to try and advertise with just flat, two dimensional print adverts. That kind of media just seems to be dying a death rattle."

– Stuart Knight, X-Taster.com

The massive uptake of sites like MySpace due to their convergent implementation of communicative technologies in one easy-to-navigate package has also brought with it another layer of impact, and one that has brought the big boys in. When MySpace introduced the ability to sign up as a band, and to add favourite songs to your profile, it further enriched the experience of its users. There's good and bad sides to all this, and currently everyone's scurrying madly about to make sense of it. There have certainly been careers launched and enhanced through MySpace and its networks: some of these tales are genuinely true, and quite a few are products of half-truths and hype from a world and its media seeking quickly to mesh in with the new revolution.

I Definitely Think Me And Tila Had A Deep Connection Here

Possibly the first, and certainly the most-referenced, success story of MySpace is the speedy rise of model and musician Tila Tequila. Born in Singapore in 1981 as Tila Nguyen,[73] before relocating first to Texas and then LA, Tila's career – and her life in general – have benefited greatly from social networking sites, being, as she firmly is, part of the net-savvy generation.

"When I was 17, 18-years-old," she says, "there were niche sites like Asianavenue.com and Black Planet that were specifically made for the Asian community or the African-American community. And I was on *every single website!* Every time I started a profile, even back then on all those sites, I was always the most popular girl that had a presence. It was weird – I think I was born into the internet zone!"

Tila's early focus, like many others, was on building a network on Friendster both for professional and personal reasons. It wasn't a satisfying experience. "I was always on there," sighs the *Playboy* model, "but for some reason – I don't know why – they kept kicking me off; there was a five hundred friend limit and I had all these fans who kept wanting to be my friend."

"Tom Anderson saw that Friendster kept deleting me; he searched me out and said, 'Well, why don't you join MySpace? We'll never kick you off, you can do whatever you want.' He pretty much knows a lot of the more powerful, influential MySpacers in real life, because it's part of his business. It's good to know these people, you know what I mean? One way or another. I was so upset about Friendster that I mass-emailed thirty thousand people to join MySpace. So I had already started off with like thirty thousand friends from my fan mailing list, right away."

That thirty thousand very quickly blossomed into its current 1.5 million; it's important to highlight here that these are people who are not just drawn toward the racy pictures or her music, but also to the *idea* of Tila herself. Her openness in posting occasionally intimate blogs and missives about her personal life enable a much more rounded insight into her life, love and career; in short, the fans feel they are communicating directly with their heroine – and pal.

"Let's say you start a profile, you write about yourself, and you just so happen to do music," continues Tila, rumpling her nose in thought. "So you say, 'Hey, I'm a musician,' right? So it's just me, talking about my life, I don't use it to always spam people, and that's what they like about me, I guess: getting to know me, personally. They know everything about me and when I go out and fans notice me, they'll comment on something very personal about me that they know. Instead of saying, 'Oh, I'm such a big fan!' they'll ask me about little things, like, 'Did you ever find your hat?!' Cause I posted a blog saying, 'Where's my fucking hat?!' So it's very personal, but at the same time I feel like they're rooting for me to be even more successful. Cause it's like, 'Hey, that's my friend. You know, I talk to her.'"

"People on MySpace used to be more, 'I'm only adding people I know,'" concludes ~~The Future Mrs Shooman~~ Miss Tequila. "I've always wanted to do music, but as with anyone else, you move from Texas to LA – where do you start? At the time I was modelling already so it's like, 'Hey, why not use modelling to build a fanbase, capitalise off of that, and then use it to promote music once I get it together on the music end.' So then

I started a band. I mean, I did all this before MySpace, but MySpace definitely helped me cross over to all fanbases worldwide. I needed to promote my career. And then people saw how it worked for me, so everyone started using MySpace that way."[74]

As I said, people like to be sold *to* and not sold *at*. This unique use of the MySpace bulletins and blogs to communicate directly with Tila's fans is one of the site's most influential features, and one which the music industry has been keen to mesh in with.

Sign 'Ere, Mate; No Need To Read That Stuff

Originally, in those pesky Terms and Conditions that nobody ever reads because they're too keen to click through all the warning pages on their way to ~~porn~~ main site content, section 6 of MySpace's T&Cs was an inadvertent ambiguity that then caused a bit of a flap.

Social commentator, folk rocker, independent spirit and all-round top geezer Billy Bragg was the person who brought this tricksy piece of legalese to the world's attention.

"Basically, and to be perfectly honest with you," begins Bragg, "I didn't really suss what MySpace was; it was Sarah in our office who said, 'This is a really good thing; we should have a presence on here.' And I said to her, 'Fine, if you want to do that, that's fine by me – but I'm writing a book, so I can't deal with this right now. But if you think it's a good idea – top, let's do it.'

So I gave her the green light on it and off she went and
set it up early in 2006, maybe in March or April."

So far, so good: a nice way to get your music out to
people and let 'em know what you're up to. But the
fireworks were about to be lit.

"I was in New York doing some shows, in late
March," continues the Essex-Londoner. "I met a friend
of mine there whose name is Sue-Ellen Stroum and
she'd started to manage an artist. I think we might have
mentioned a bit about MySpace and she subsequently
went on to establish a MySpace presence for her artist, a
mate of mine called Fionn O'Lochlainn. Being
a conscientious manager, she read the Terms and
Conditions."

Aha! So someone actually does…

"When she read them she then emailed our office to ask me if this could be real," Bragg says, "that they [appear to be] asking for a worldwide, royalty-free licence; and if it is real, what does it mean? So the office then got in touch and said, 'Um, MySpace are [asking for] a worldwide, royalty-free licence!' And I said, 'Well, that can't be right. I can't have that.' Cause I own my rights; I only lease them to record labels for the duration of the deal, so I'm pretty strict about who gets rights to my material. I said, 'That can't be right' and the office checked it out, and [on the surface] it was. I said, 'Well, we can't have stuff on there; we have to pull our stuff off then.' So we pulled our stuff off, pulled the music off but kept the presence, and just let everybody know why we'd done this, [saying] we were suspending putting any music on there until this was resolved, or *clarified*. I got a surprising number of emails from people saying, 'I didn't think of this before, I hadn't read the Terms and Conditions, this obviously can't be right.' And as these things do on the internet, word got out to some of the online music mags who started asking me about it, and it eventually percolated its way through to the mainstream media. It blew up very, very fast, much to my surprise really."

The prolific writer began speaking to – and writing in – the music media on this issue.

"I wrote an article for *Music Week* on MySpace, in the middle of June. Basically, it was calling on MySpace to either modify or clarify, based on their proprietary rights and content clause, which I thought was pretty tight terms. What I wanted them to clarify was who they believed owned the sole right to exploit the content put on MySpace, and to make it explicit in their terms of agreement who they believed owned it."

"Within a week, literally, of that appearing in *Music Week*, they modified their T&Cs to what I think they still are now. Their proprietary rights clause, which is Number Six, it now begins with [words to the effect of], 'You are the owner of the work that you put on here.'"

Nice work BB.

"They didn't change the rights that they demanded. They still demand that you grant to MySpace a non-exclusive, royalty-free licence. But what they did was, instead of just saying that it now says that the licence you grant to MySpace is non-exclusive [meaning you are free to licence your content to anyone else in addition to MySpace, fully paid and royalty free, meaning that MySpace is not required to pay *you* for the use on MySpace services of the content that you post]. So, they've clarified it and made it clear that they're not talking about owning the rights to do what they want to do with it. It [clarifies clearly], and this is the most important thing I think, that MySpace.com does not claim any ownership rights in the text files, images, blah blah blah blah blah, that you post on MySpace. After posting your content on MySpace you continue to own all ownership rights of such content, and you have the right to use your content any way you choose."

Much better.

"That was what I wanted," Billy ponders. "A clear statement of where they believe ownership lies. I happen to think now that the MySpace proprietary rights clause is a pretty good starting point for a clause. Because it also has a get-out clause: licence terminates any time you remove your content from MySpace services. This licence does not grant MySpace the right to sell your content, nor does the licence grant MySpace the right to distribute your content outside the MySpace services. I mean, that to me is fine; if that had been in the original proprietary rights clause I don't think there would have been a problem: because it's clear."

"What I'm trying to avoid," Bragg concludes, "is not only people [losing out], but also trying to make sure that people can utilise the full potential of MySpace, which I think is an incredible potential, without having to sit down with a lawyer every time they want to put something on there. That to me is totally contrary to the spirit of the internet, and to the spirit of MySpace. So I am very pleased with the way they've changed that now. I think the change they made reflects much more now the spirit of the internet, which is what MySpace has built itself on; whoever it was that decided to change and rewrite that proprietary rights clause I think stayed true to the spirit of the founders of MySpace. People recognise that they're getting a free service but by the same token they don't deserve to [have] their rights [messed with]. The clarifications are really good, I think, because you now understand what they're doing. And why they need these rights – and that makes sense."

It does indeed. Sorted. Get it?

MySpace Makes Things Happen For Bands

"You could see it building," says former gig promoter and current hot-property in digital and viral marketing, Sammy Andrews. "From the off, there weren't that many bands on MySpace when it started. And I did take the time, when people were asking me, to get into it."

"The initial thing I did when I was promoting was that I went and found four thousand people who lived in Newcastle who wanted to go to a gig. And I saw returns straight away. Right from the start, MySpace had the search feature where you could put in a postcode and find a little bit about people, age, sex and location. When I had a rock night I would go and invite all the rock fans. It was working; we ran competitions through it and promotions, and had instant feedback. So from then, as well as having the web page on the flyers we had the MySpace page address."

"We had a forum on the venue's own website which was always very active, but as soon as the MySpace page went up the forum was active every day with people from outside Newcastle that had come in. I could see what it was going to do just from a venue point of view. It's exactly the same technique that I use with bands now. You want to find the right people and do the right things: it's the same principle. It's done that from the start even when it didn't have all the features on it."

"In terms of Hot Club de Paris," agrees Paul Rafferty, vocalist and bassist for said quirkyjumpyhuggysexy pop band, "we tend to use the site as a barometer. We've never actively added friends – apart from when we first started our MySpace page and added our close friends and bands we liked to play with. Friend requests and song plays indicate the level of exposure you're receiving; either through the press or through playing live in support of bigger bands. We like MySpace because it keeps us directly in touch with people who have chosen to keep an eye on what we're doing. It's essentially a mailing list with pictures and music. It's become an essential tool."

Building connections; building social networks.
People *talking to each other*.

How The Musick Industry Started Going, 'Ere, Wot's All This About Then?'

"It was one of those names that was knocking about the *NME* office in the way that new band names knock about the *NME* office," muses the magazine's editor, Conor McNicholas. "So we were kinda aware of it, and then came that 'MySpace explosion', and for every A&R man the real measure about how exciting a band was, was how many friends they had on MySpace. This is before all the kind of mass music PR corruption that has started to creep in, when it was vaguely pure! An independent arbiter of how good, or how exciting this music was. And it was tremendously exciting for everybody for a while."

Not least for the bands; the massive surge of new music available on the site during 2005 and 2006 really did provide a more level playing field for acts seeking to break through some of the barriers that existed between their music and the A&R departments of record labels. This also applied to reaching out to Radio One DJs including Huw Stephens, whose influential show on that station is entirely dependent on first discovering and subsequently playing records by new, unknown bands.

"For me, personally it's become invaluable," y mae o'n dweud.[75] "Two years ago, all the music I received was through the post. I try and listen to everything that comes in, whether it's a CD or MySpace, but the volume of stuff coming through MySpace is just so much at the

moment that I can't keep up! But in terms of finding out about bands and what other music they like, which other bands they feel an affinity to in their area, seeing their gig dates or just hearing the music, plus getting in touch with the bands – and the bands getting in touch with me – well, instead of mailing a BBC address which I might not check every day, cause I'm not in work every day, people get in touch with me through MySpace and I do check that every day."

"It's made it so easy to contact bands and friends," parhauodd yr DJ. "You MySpace them, you Google them, it's made getting in touch with people – music-wise or socially – so, so easy. It's unbelievable really. It's like a mobile phone, kind of, what did you do before you had one? What did you do *in a world before MySpace*! We've booked sessions for the show through MySpace – bypassing pluggers and management."

Daily Star music journalist Joe Mott agrees. "I'll always click on and have a look," he says, "and if I like it I'll stick 'em on as a mate and read anything else, with interest, that they post to me. It does give you the potential to hear a lot of bands and a lot of music that you wouldn't hear necessarily, even if you were going out more traditionally, to gigs of unsigned bands. Cause anyone can get on there you will hear a lot more – a lot more of it's shit as well – but a lot more will get through there, which is I guess why all the A&Rs are using it so much. As an A&R tool."

"I can't give them a record deal," Motty[76] continues, "But if I want to I can write about them. I haven't had to have an A&R man to discover them, to sign them and then to employ some press people to let me know about them. Immediately I can hear, you know, Larry and his

85

boys in Scunthorpe, find out what they're about and what they can do. If I hear it and it makes me think, 'Fuck me, that's amazing', I'll write about it."

"In terms of direct access it feels less remote than the official sites," offers *Billboard* magazine's Mark Sutherland, "because generally those are put together by the record company, and they've got a keen interest in selling you something, generally speaking – or at least directing you somewhere where you can buy something. Whereas MySpace, whether it's true or not, is very good at giving the illusion that here you are in direct contact with that band; that there is no third party obscuring your access to them; that this is the truth from the horse's mouth."

Arctic Monkeys' online PR is handled by Serena Wilson of Nile-On; there's nobody better to sum it up than she.

"What I think about MySpace," she says, "is that it's in your hands again. It's in the people's hands; it's no longer about what someone is telling you to wear, or to eat, or to listen to – it's about what *you* want. And actually, getting music in the traditional way – which is through your peers. It's very rare that someone will go to a site and search for a band on their own. But you've got all these friends online and they're listening to music, so you're finding out about music traditionally."

We are talking about momentum here: finding like-minded people – peer groups – and giving them a forum in which to congregate; initially digitally through a social networking site, and subsequently at gigs in real life. If there's one thing that brings people together more than anything else, it's a shared love of music. And as MySpace became a household word in the morning tabloids, several bands' seemingly overnight rises to fame have been inextricably linked with the rise of the site itself.

But, as Tony Wilson says, "That big moment when the British media went mad about it two months ago was *pure fucking bollocks.*"

Here's a couple of those 'success stories' told in the words of those who know what *really* happened. And maybe a bit of swearing if I can shoehorn it in somewhere.

Arctic Monkeys, Schmarctic Schmonkeys

"Traditionally, bands toured cities and played every venue possible to create buzz about their music," says Serena Wilson of Nile-On PR, "but with MySpace, bands can host demos of their songs, announce shows and connect with fans without spending weeks on the road. Some bands make the mistake of thinking that they can create a MySpace page and just *be in MySpace,* in this virtual world, when actually it's increasingly more important as your fanbase and your profile grows on MySpace that your fans can physically have contact with you as well. And a lot of artists make the mistake that it's just going to be down to MySpace in gaining those fans:

but once you've gained those fans, what do you do with them? They want to see you perform."

"It's a great way of getting attention," agrees Mark Sutherland, "but you're not gonna actually become internationally famous and successful just because you've got a lot of friends on MySpace. It doesn't work that way, sadly, and it probably never will. But in a world where the music business is ever more concerned with making money fast, ever less keen to make long-term investments in people, then it's a useful tool for you as a band if you can generate buzz quickly, and the music industry's always going to be interested in capitalising on that."

Indeed they are. And in the case of Sheffield band Arctic Monkeys, 2006 saw their star firmly in the ascendant. The popular reading of the tale goes something like this: Band starts. Band starts MySpace page. Band suddenly magically has sixty five thousand friends and millions of page views. Band gets dead famous and tours to packed crowds at huge venues. *And it's all down to MySpace.com!*

Is it?

Remember what Tony Wilson said a page or two back? If you've forgotten, just ~~hit the 'back' button on your browser~~ use your 'fingers' to 'turn over the pages'.

"It wasn't MySpace," declares Stuart Knight. "No. They'd already played Reading Festival! They'd already

headlined the Astoria. I went to that show, before any of this happened, and then of course the album came out. And because everyone was starved for released material, they all went out and bought it. I think MySpace was kinda *there*. MySpace is a great tool if you're a new artist and you want someone to hear your music; it's a great place to park it. You can forward your MySpace address and get people to download the songs."

"Arctic Monkeys were obviously doing incredibly well on the first album which made everyone think 'what is this site doing?'" expands Stuart Clarke, Talent Editor of the music trade bible, *Music Week*. "The fact of the matter is that MySpace, or online in general, played a very small part in that band's development and the development of their fanbase. They'd be on the road for eighteen months, just touring and touring in every little dive that they could get to – which was much more important to their ultimate success than the site was. As is now pretty common knowledge they never actually – and still don't – have an official MySpace page. It's always just been fans setting up their own pages for them. Tribute pages, you know?" Because you never know who's who online, remember?

Serena Wilson: "Arctic Monkeys were playing every small dive that there was, and giving demos away at their gigs, which kids then went back home and uploaded onto MySpace. And that's the way that their music got around – it wasn't just about their MySpace page although they were giving lots of music away. They were happy for the kids to have the music, to do what they wanted and to pass the music around amongst themselves. They also had so much interaction with the fans; at a very early stage they were in there chatting to their fans. Traditionally, that was never possible; the ability to connect directly with artists is just part of the attraction of MySpace, the closest you could get to an artist in the past was a meet and greet or stand at a stage door hoping for a glimpse. Basically it wasn't so easy for fans to have that interaction with their idols, if you like. MySpace has really brought to the forefront how important that is."

"At the end of the day the music will speak for itself. They had good music, they had good tracks, and it was evident when you went to their gigs before they'd released anything – they weren't even signed yet to Domino – and the kids were singing along from their *guts*. You could feel it in the air; there was a real buzz about them. There's no way it wouldn't have happened – they are an amazing band."

Joe Mott: "People seem to forget that they were doing the gigs, and they had the loyal fanbase already. They had, as far as I can tell, a fanbase as big as Babyshambles had, before they got picked up by the tabloids and became immense. Then that fanbase took it to the net as well, which helped it spread: but they'd already done the hard graft. If they didn't have the fanbase then it wouldn't have mattered whether they were on the internet. I don't actually believe that there's yet been a band that's been 'made' on the internet."

Mark Sutherland: "I saw them live, early on, and their gig was packed with people singing along to every word of songs that hadn't been released. They were probably the big sensations of Reading Festival 2005, playing a tiny tent that you couldn't get anywhere near if you just turned up after they'd come on, because there were so many thousands of people who'd come to see them. And yet none of their media coverage really kicked in until they'd had a number one record."

"The key thing with the Arctic Monkeys's success story, to me, is that they were a good, old-fashioned, grass-roots British music scene success story. Where the internet proved influential was the fact that it just accelerated everything. I have no doubt that Arctic Monkeys would have got to Number One in the charts eventually. I have no doubt that they would have sold a lot of records eventually. Perhaps the most obvious predecessor to them is the Stone Roses, but they took years and years to build up a following like that, playing live, and you'd hear reports from up in the north about how there were hundreds of fans squeezing into their gigs; then eventually people would check it out and there's this long, slow process. The internet just accelerated it vastly. I think the media was looking for a way to justify the fact that they had missed the Arctic Monkeys coming up, because they hadn't had the sort of coverage you'd expect in the sort of places for a band like that who were fairly obviously on the rise."

"MySpace was in the ascendant at the same time as the Arctic Monkeys," offers Sam Sparrow, head of digital content at Warner Music. "So people just stuck them both together."

"Generally there is a lot of media spin about MySpace," says Conor McNicholas of *NME*. "When the Arctic Monkeys first broke big, the media was desperate to talk about MySpace, but actually MySpace had pretty much bugger all to do with it. It was about kids swapping MP3s in chat forums, but it wasn't anything to do with MySpace and the platform that it gives. It was part of it, but it wasn't really what had driven it, and initially it was done with driving backwards and forwards and playing lots of very small gigs and handing out free CDs. And that's the kind of stuff that people had been doing for years previously. But I think it was just an excuse for the media — suddenly they had a name to put to MySpace, because they knew it was important, but they didn't know how to talk about it."

The Arctic Monkeys weren't 'broken', then, by MySpace. Perhaps it had a part in a bigger picture, and certainly the site is user-friendly in the sense that its easy navigation and relatively straightforward music player make it simple to check out bands — and if you like what you hear, add them as a friend. This self-propagating network building is the basis of MySpace's success, and its explosion into the world's popular consciousness.

But to say this band owes its success purely to MySpace... well.

Turn back to that Tony Wilson quote.

Lily Allen

As we're on this media myth-busting crusade, what about Lily Allen? She was broken by MySpace, wasn't she? Well, not really; there's a little more to it than that. Let's talk Lily. Or, more specifically, let's hear Jamie Nelson talk about Lily. Jamie is an A&R executive at her label, Parlophone. He knows lots of cool stuff, which you're about to read after this sentence finishes.

"It would be very easy to give you a very romantic message of the A&R process being a MySpace thing," begins Nelson, immediately after the rather spurious preceding sentence finished, "and it really wasn't like that. Lily, from stage one, has always been absolutely, brilliantly self-aware about what she is. Obviously for all of us it's great to get feedback on how people like your music. Ultimately the vision for the songs, and the focus, and all that stuff, had happened long before she'd set that page up. The recordings that you hear on the record now, give or take the odd mix, are pretty much the same as what they were a year ago when we did the deal. The actual A&R process, even, was comparatively painless – just because what she originally delivered was so great-sounding. So it wasn't a great case of her posting up tracks and then changing them because of comments or anything like that, there was never any element of that to it; it's just obviously quite reassuring when you post up songs of yours anywhere. It's no different to playing music to people and getting great feedback on tracks you feel were great in the first place. It's that sort of thing."[77]

"I do feel like she would have had success as an artist in general because as a musician, without sounding too ridiculous, her voice resonates with her generation in a certain way. And what she has to say connects with people of her own age group and I think that's partly where her success lies. MySpace specifically is a format that's relevant today. It's another tag, an additional thing to where media is, an additional opportunity for people to get a flavour of what somebody's personality is like. In a relatively easy way. I don't see it like, 'without MySpace it wouldn't have happened for Lily,' but it certainly gave people an easy format to get a full vibe on what she's like as a personality, and of course to hear the brilliant music that she delivers."

"I think from an A&R perspective, you know what it's like, people start to lose the plot on some of these things and I think if what you were making was really shit music, that was unappealing and uninteresting, you can post it wherever you want and nobody's gonna get particularly excited about it. It only becomes interesting and relevant and important if what you're doing is unusual and clever and engaging and exciting. And then of course people want to know about it – and it doesn't matter what format it gets seen on or how people get an opportunity to be exposed to it; at that second they connect to it. And ultimately that's no different than it would have been fifty years ago."

"I think we were up to 1.5 million hits on Lily's MySpace before the album was out. We've not sold a million and a half albums off the back of it. It's not like for like, if that makes sense. But all the same it's been a really positive thing; it's a good thing for her to have had and I think it's obviously been a really interesting thing for us."

Mark Sutherland: "Lily Allen had a record deal before she had a MySpace site. So somebody had already spotted her potential as an artist. So it's great if you're a PR. But it's great if you're a journalist, if somebody says, 'this band have got this many friends' then you think that's at least a degree of popularity. You're not so much taking a shot in the dark as perhaps you would have been in the old days, when you would have to take a gamble on a band, get behind them and support them in terms of press coverage. This way at least you think people are interested already. In a way, I think that's kind of removed the A&R function of music journalism a bit, which is a shame. But it means they're taking less risks."

There's also the deep connection that the fans feel with the artists that certainly is engendered by the social networking aspect of MySpace. Joe Mott pertinently points out that, "there's always that hope that if you click on Lily Allen's MySpace page and ask 'Can I be your friend', every time you go back to your MySpace you've that hope: 'Is she going to accept it?' Can you imagine the buzz if she did, if you're really into her and it's your thing as a 14/15/16/17-year-old kid? Cause I know I'd be sat there thinking: Well, Lily did that, I know it was Lily: she saw my name, she saw my thing, she checked out my MySpace and said, 'Yeah. I'm gonna be his mate.' And that adds a whole other level of contact with the celeb/artist/band that you're a fan of. And it certainly beats a signed CD or an autograph if you've a live connection that says, 'YES! I'm gonna accept you as a friend!' And I think the wording is important as well: 'so and so has put in a friend request, do you accept?' – 'Yes, I accept you as my friend.' It means a lot, certainly to a teenager."

I Think I Tried To Chat Sandi Up Once, Now I Come To Think Of It [78]

2006 also saw the rise of Scottish singer/songwriter Sandi Thom. Although Sandi's tale is obliquely related to MySpace, it is certainly worth looking at because it highlights not only the way that online promotion has exploded, but how the media – if not the record buyers themselves – has bought into it.

Sandi's story goes a little like this: unknown, pert guitarist and singer is broke. She is based in London and spending all her time and cash travelling round in a bashed-up ol' motor-chugga, playing her accessible ditties in pubs and clubs all over the UK. But she is broke. So she gets the idea of touring the UK without leaving her Tooting basement. She sets up a webcam and performs, amongst the spiders and the slime, twenty one nights in succession, making the 'virtual gigs' accessible on the web and promoting them through MySpace. The first performance garners four hundred viewers; the twenty-first is seen by over a hundred thousand. Sandi then releases her breakthrough single, which gets to Number One in the Pop Charts. *And it's all down to MySpace!*

Here's Mr. Wilson again: "Sandi Thom, 'the girl that had done her own webcast, and it was a do-it-yourself thing' – she signed a huge bloody publishing deal. Publishing's the most important aspect of a music deal; it's where all the real money is – and her publishers, they were paying for a proper website webcast. So there is a lot of bollocks about it."

I love that man, and if he lets me, I'm going to take him down Rusholme way and buy him the best curry in the world.

Korda Marshall, Head Of Warner UK: "Sandi Thom didn't have a server big enough to deal with all the 125,000 people who downloaded her video. So it's not all done out of a bedroom in Stockwell or Camden, it's done with the backup and the full services of a major corporation with all the facilities and ISP, and all the digital know-how that you need to make that work."

"That Sandi Thom thing was a totally marketed thing, wasn't it, basically?" says Huw Stephens. "The same thing as Arctic Monkeys in that there's people pro-actively pushing them through the internet – but they're just using that MySpace site as an extra tool in the whole campaign."

As it turns out, of course, Sandi was already well on the way to inking a deal with RCA[79]; her management had already set up a publishing deal with Windswept, who also boast Beyonce Knowles as an artist on their books. A million e-flyers had been sent out via the web and Sandi's own MySpace site; the servers were provided by Streaming Tank, a company specialising in bandwidth. That the media bought into a good story is nothing new. And, because MySpace was hot to trot, it was another easy mash-together for tomorrow's chip wrappers.[80]

Joe Mott: "Of course it's a complete publicity stunt, but – so what? I've got no problem with that. Again, it was being used as a tool. Is it any worse than, say, spending a load of money to take journalists somewhere flash, and giving them a great light show, or something, you know? Or – and I like her – pouring a load of money into promoting Amy Winehouse's album to make sure it sells 300,000? I mean, if you look at Lily Allen, for example, her album's selling for £6 in Virgin. They're not making any money on that album. So I don't see any harm in using the internet, or MySpace, or whatever they are claiming it is for Sandi Thom. It's another tool out there; it's hot; so let's just copy it. It's free to do, and if muggins journalists will buy it and write about it, well – why not?"

Why not indeed? The marketing of acts through the web has become an integral part of any band's career; contrasting this with the situation ten years ago is fun, so let's do that for a bit.

Contrasting MySpace With The Situation Ten Years Ago For Fun

"Social networks like MySpace allow people to find music online in the same way they find out about music in person through their peers," declares Serena Wilson of online PR company Nile-On. "Very few people go to a website looking for bands they've never heard of before. In the early stages, a lot of artists/labels we worked with were wary of social networks and using MySpace, they didn't get it or weren't that interested. They wanted coverage on AOL or MSN. Nowadays artists won't let us near their MySpace pages to manage them. They are addicted and use it for all sorts of networking and contacts. I was disillusioned by the whole Friendster network. The people I wanted to meet weren't signed up; it was the people from school that you didn't like that were online! So MySpace coming along with a credible background to it was fresh blood. Especially for the music industry; there wasn't anything really like it out there."

"When I started, labels and artists were so – not negative – but so uninterested in the internet and MySpace," she continues. "The Monkeys was just one campaign that changed that, and was instrumental in getting people to take note of the possibilities of sites like MySpace. I've been working in online since 1999 and it's taken this long to get to where we are. The independent labels have always been more forthcoming with ideas and giving away free music, but eventually they have to get bolder. It seems clear that the only way for the majors to stay on top of the music industry into the next decade is to take more risks – both technological and creative – than they have done for a long time. The majors have been much slower in embracing certain aspects of the internet."

Peter Croxson is in charge of Feeder's online street teaming and web promotion. A massive fan of the band, he soon became directly involved in spreading the word about Feeder through their website, which in a cunning stunt is called Feederweb. In the olden days, getting the digital word out was a little more of a palaver.[81]

"Initially it was an email group of various people who were from the official message boards," says Peter. "Emails were going round saying, 'We've got a single coming out this week, can you email radio stations and TV video channels, asking them to play the song.' From that point it expanded to a few more people, which eventually formed into yet another message board where members of the street team would congregate to get news, and were set tasks to promote various things."

"The problem with band emails is that they often go into a spam folder," continues Croxson. "The Sign Up enables you to set up a mailing list, but the email address it comes from is basically a load of numbers. Most internet-based email, or even Outlook Express, will treat that as spam because it doesn't recognise the sender as a word, and therefore you might not see it. Whereas with something like MySpace it's always gonna come from a central email address, and it should go into someone's inbox. And you can send something out immediately; with MySpace you can send out a bulletin or a new blog, and if people are subscribed to it, it's pushed out to them and you're not relying on people coming to your own site to look things up."

Cause it brings together all the communications possibilities into one easy package, innit.

"My opinions have totally changed round in the space of six months," concludes Croxson. "Initially, I assumed MySpace was for dating and networking, and that bands didn't really have much of a place on there. When I first started there were two or three thousand friends but having developed it and tapped into the potential, it's now pushing the eighteen thousand mark and we get thirty or forty requests a day. And I'm not doing anything and the band aren't doing anything to push that: it's just via people searching through it, finding it, looking at the page and getting interested enough to want to be a friend and feel part of it. You could previously have a band website – Feederweb has existed since 1998 – but unless people found it and were aware of the band, they wouldn't have seen it, whereas with MySpace there's a search facility where you can search for bands and listen to the tracks and get involved that way. There was no involvement with a bog standard website and really there still isn't. There is Feeder Central where you can log in and get exclusive content, but generally that content is also now put onto the MySpace page, in the blog and so on."

"For me, as an artist, it certainly brings me a lot closer to my audience," says Billy Bragg. "People can leave me messages on there, and when I've got time I can respond directly to them. I could do that on my Billy Bragg website. The Billy Bragg website is like a gig, and MySpace is like a festival; there's a lot of other people on MySpace swanning around, you know, following clues that normally wouldn't necessarily come to billybragg.co.uk. People in the MySpace community who want to check out what I'm doing can come through that; they're already in the loop. So it has great potential and if I were an artist just starting out now I think I would see it as a really good tool to use. Previously in order to get some peer-approval I would've needed to have learnt to play an instrument and written songs, which you have to do anyway, but then I would have had to get gigs where I could bring an audience along. Well, you can kind of cultivate an audience on MySpace. That's one of the real interesting aspects of social networking sites. Whether that can then feed through into a career, we're finding that out at the moment. We'll learn that."

We will indeed.

Exclusive Content + Credibility = Sales?

"Word of mouth is the new word of mouth," smiles Sammy Andrews. "Adverts haven't got the same impact. Because they've conditioned us over the years, there's so much advertising now that we as a generation have learnt to block it out. I know they're trying to ban child advertising on telly but we block it out now anyway. And any kid that's been on the internet over a year knows to block popups. That was something very early on with the internet that I hated, where you go on a site and you're bombarded by all these popups and people were paying a fortune to have them placed there. It's pointless. When you click on them accidentally, you hate that you've spent five minutes trying to get out of it. It's not the same thing."

"But kids are talking amongst themselves now, and rather than discussing something with your mate in the playground, from a music perspective, rather than giving your mate a tape, they're discussing it online with someone from the other side of the world that they've never met. There's a generation of kids who are staying in more and more, and from my point of view, a generation where there's a lot of fear being bred outside your own home. Everyone's a little nervous about things, ASBOS, whatever, but people are spending more and more time at home and minority groups are moving forward. Any minority group's getting bigger in every country. You can find people like *you* on the internet, and they're spending hours and hours talking, exchanging things. It's changing the world, I think, that they can talk about anything they want, they can talk amongst each other and something can now spread across the seas without having to be bought for millions of pounds."

How The Musick Industry Can Make MySpace Do Very Interesting Stuff, And That

"I came up with an idea for the band Xpress-2," says David Rowell of Bigger Picture Media, who previously worked as marketing director at the record label, Echo. "That band had a track called Kill 100 so we thought we'd do a hundred remixes."

Broadband's fast enough to do that these days; firing files about is, of course, more prevalent than ever before, and there's a generation who've grown up knowing little else in Internet-land. So getting a hundred remixes for a track was finally possible; networks within networks on sites like MySpace allowed a groundswell of interest to form.

"We put the separate musical parts up on kill100.com," continues Rowell, "allowed people four to six weeks to put their mix together and submit it. We had a thousand mixes come back which we got down to a shortlist of three hundred and then 108."

"Now, if I'd been calculating, in my marketing way, I could have chosen those people with the biggest MySpace presence. But I didn't. We actually chose what we considered to be the best mixes. But the idea was that then each of those remixers – and this is all chart eligible – would enter into a competition where the one that had the most pre-orders by the Saturday of release week would get £2,000 for their mix. It was just a really interesting thing to do."

Clever, too. And it worked.

"Firstly, I didn't think we'd get a hundred mixes," Rowell ponders. "The fact we got three hundred was just fantastic. The fact that three *thousand* registered their interest showed that there was an anticipation for that band. Having a band with a profile obviously helps."

But you didn't need MySpace for that, did you? Or even the web itself, if you extrapolate it to the fullest, like.

"The interesting thing," Rowell smiles, "is that 80% of those people had a MySpace page, and were pushing out their message to their MySpacers. This was part of my plan. 'OK, let's think what these people do: they regularly DJ, so they've probably got a database of sorts.'

You know, it was trying to harness all these additional pieces. Now I would say that probably 30% of them really entered into the spirit of it, 50% just wanted to be associated with the band and tell their mates that they'd remixed Xpress-2, and the other 20% were saying, 'How dare you to ask us to go and sell our own mix!?' But it just proves that the whole idea I had was spurred on by the nature of MySpace: 'OK there's a massive shop window here,' and this is, again, in a sense, part of the good and the bad. I wouldn't call it a groundbreaking idea, but it was an idea which was able to evolve cause of a great social forum round it. But, equally, none of these things will work perfectly; unless you're completely calculated in the way you do it. And then you will inevitably lose quality. We went for quality over quantity – and, as I say, it worked OK."

"From my point of view, if we're turning remixer into retailer," concludes Rowell, "it's just informing me about what that transition is like, and how people find that situation. The interesting thing is that some of these things don't mix, and no amount of research will tell you if it's right or wrong. You know, if you search hard enough you'll find a hundred people who want to do it. We managed to put this whole competition together for £300, but I spent probably fifteen hundred man-hours doing it and answering four hundred emails a day. But that was part of the process and, to be honest with you, it was a massive learning experience. I've been doing this job a long time. You come up with ambitious projects and ways of marketing records, and doing this, that and the other, but I'd never come up with something on that scale before. I would certainly do it again, but probably not as big as that."

"I do think we'll be able to call upon the MySpacers, who inevitably have their own MySpace pages, to go out and spread the word. And it incentivises them to not only build a database, but you always have to weigh it up, know what you need to achieve. With Kill 100 it was more about seeing how all the parts joined together. I'd been having conversations with EMI and they put a site together that Brian Eno and David Byrne had done, ironically after his Xpress-2 thing. And it cost them £100,000 I think! It cost us £1500. But theirs didn't necessarily need the man-hours put into it. We did a league and there was a real-time solution, so as soon as someone bought one of the mixes it went up in the league – it was a sort of competitive spirit we tried to inject into it. I wouldn't say it worked perfectly but it was a real eye-opener for me."

The concept of blurring the boundaries between fan, remixer, band, retailer and record company is, without a doubt, one of the fundamental building blocks of Web 2.0. MySpace is a tool in the whole process, but cannot – and should not – be thought of as a one-stop solution. As in the cases outlined here, bands still need to get out there and sell records; they still need to hit radio and print media, and they still need to gather fans to come and see them at gigs. There's a strong case to be made that merchandise sales will provide bands with the finance lost from other, more traditional revenue streams, but it's beyond the remit of this book.[82]

"The mainstream media will use it as a buzzword," says Daryl Bamonte. "They'll just go, 'MySpace did it' and you're supposed to think that it's just this kid in their bedroom but it's not; you find out if you scratch beneath the surface that, whilst it is the kind of 'in thing', they're still doing loads of gigs and have got a publicist. But it's just a different route, rather than relying on the inky press or whatever."

"I really do like it," enthuses the ex-manager of The Cure. "It takes us back to the origins of the internet[83] that you can instantly get through a lot of barriers because, in a lot of ways, it's opened up the bigger artists to the people. I think a lot of times, artists are quite receptive to ideas that might sound a bit quirky at first but maybe there's a filter system. For Robert Smith, I like to think I always passed on everything because that's what he liked me to do. I'm sure other people maybe have an involuntary filter system so it doesn't necessarily get through to them. MySpace makes everybody more accessible to each other. It stripped away a lot of bollocks about the internet, which became a huge – not dishonest – but a sleazy, money-spinning kind of thing. That's why I liked MySpace, because it stripped it back to what was good about it."

Thus sweeping away, of course, The Viagra Years.

"I've been working with a band, Scarling, from LA for a year and a half," concludes Bamonte. "They've got fifty thousand friends; this is a band who's just signed to an indie label in California. When we were doing shows last year and this year in the UK, we would notice a spike in ticket sales just from doing a MySpace mailout, or just a posting."

"If you've got a band that's big and has a huge mailing list it's good but if you've got a huge promoter behind them and the funds to pay for TV advertising or maybe print advertising, then you're not necessarily going to be able to pinpoint whether it was down to something like a mailing list mailout, cause it might coincide with a big advert in Q magazine the same week. But when you've got a band who haven't really got other outlets, it's very noticeable; we'd do a MySpace mailout then there'd be a very big spike. So I think it's proven that for bands that maybe don't have many other backup facilities to promote themselves it definitely works."

And it does, to a point. That said, the amount of smoke and mirrors about the perceived part that MySpace and sites like it have played in the career-building of bands is staggering, tiresome and I'm going to stop talking about it after this sentence finishes, unless I think of something else a bit later in the book, which is entirely possible.[84]

I Told You This Book Was Already Obsolete, But You Didn't Listen Did You?

"People talk about the internet as another medium alongside newspapers and magazines, and it isn't really. The internet is a super-medium in the sense that it brings together a lot of other media as we understand them; things like television or radio can exist in different forms within it. MySpace, and social networking sites, are themselves a new medium. So it's rather like writing a story: 'The Arctic Monkeys – nobody had ever heard of them before they appeared on the cover of NME! NME is a magazine, magazines are really popular, they're gonna change the way we talk about bands because we can now see them as well as hear them!' It's just ridiculous. It's become just what people do – in the same way that a radio station promotes new music, MySpace promotes new music. It does it in a very different way, but I think on its own it's not a story anymore."

– Conor McNicholas, editor, *New Musical Express*

Steady on mate, there's another hundred pages to go, you swine. I s'pose you could just look at the pictures from hereon in, they're the best bit by miles.

Part Five:

What The Web Did Next

Free! Free! Free!
Now! Now! Now!
New! New! New!

One problem is that the generation that's grown up with MySpace and sites like it have also grown up with a few key concepts that sites such as Napster highlighted.

One of these is the idea that sharing music should be unregulated: once it's up there as your profile track on MySpace, for instance, everyone can hear that track when they surf to your page. Music being the social force it is, the tracks you choose as a personal signature are as powerful a statement of your own taste as the 'About Me' section or your blog about winged pooches. Clearly, however, this digital version of playground tape-swapping is something that worries a lot of people who created that content. Someone had to pay for recording and releasing these songs. Whither their recompense?[85] And does the huge turnover of bands fuelled by this new instant culture lend itself to lasting careers?

"I suppose it says something about the way music is made and distributed these days," offers *NME* editor Conor McNicholas. "MySpace just happened to be the right thing at the right time. It's all to do with the breakdown of the traditional role of the record industry as a connector between fans and bands. As the internet said, instantly, 'You don't control the means of distribution anymore', then MySpace made that even easier than ever before. So the market was absolutely ripe for it before it ever turned up."

"The thing for music fans," he continues, "is that obviously half the joy of new music is the newness. And something can only be new for a small amount of time, so if the first thing you hear about somebody is that they release an album or they release a single, then that's very exciting, and you're with them on that journey. The way it happened with Kaiser Chiefs, or Franz Ferdinand; we're only talking three years ago now, but nobody really knew who Franz Ferdinand were until they released 'Take Me Out' and it went to Number Three at a very quiet part of the year. Suddenly they'd come out of nowhere and everyone could live with them for that year."

"Nowadays, the buzz will start on a band when they've got a couple of early demos out, or the early adopter fans will get very, very excited; by the time they've got round to sorting out a manager, the manager's been round the A&R circuit and has got them a deal, you're talking six months to a year in – six months minimum – by which time everyone's going, 'God, I've been listening to this for six months!' And then they move onto something else. Nobody's going to release a record until they've booked the retail space at HMV or Virgin Megastore, and it's gonna take six months to record and get a single out of any kind, so by the time people have 'dropped' a band they end up turning up six months later and releasing a single. And everyone's going, 'God, are they still around?'"

"So, record companies have a really serious problem. I had a conversation with somebody at a record company the other day; I said, 'If I was doing your job I would be doing everything in my power to concertina that signing-to-release process, because that's really killing your industry at the moment. Cause you're not moving as fast as the fans are; you need to have things signed within weeks of it first appearing, and then get single releases out in days. And anything you have to do to make that happen is what's gonna drive your future. Cause if you run it the way you do at the moment, the fans will just walk all over you. They'll go somewhere else.'"

"Now, culturally, it is very quick," agrees Korda Marshall. "You're on your third generation of Generation X; you've got kids who've never lived through a recession; never really fought a war; they're all very well-educated; they're all very information technology-aware; they all don't like to be sold to – they like to buy their own things. Everything is louder, faster, harder, angrier, dirtier. Everything's quicker – nobody's got any patience. Nobody wants to wait to buy a house; they want to buy a house *now*! The process of wanting, it's all quick, quick, quick, quick. Everything digital, or telecoms, or MySpace-related, is all part of that culture.

Sociologically, it's a very information-aware, technology-driven generation. And they're used to finding out their own things, so they don't wanna know what Radio One are playing; they want to get their own playlist together. They don't wanna wait for the record to come out in three weeks' time; they want to get it now. And if they can get it streaming on MySpace then that's what they will do."

There is, in other words, a power shift: rather than having music and cultural cues pushed at us by traditional media and record companies, the MySpace generation will choose their own channels, their own musical heroes, and ultimately their own content. It's not the information superhighway any more, it's more like a no-holds-barred stock car smash-up in the Nevada desert, except with fewer rules and hundreds of millions of ever-faster cars. Hmm, does that work? Yeah I think it does. You know what I mean anyway.

How The Industry Learned To Stop Worrying And Love The Download

One of the huge fallacies about the concept of music being available online is that it is killing the record industry: it isn't. It's strengthening it, if anything, and thank the Lord that the customers are able to audition and choose music that is to their taste more than ever before. MySpace itself is an avatar for the new power shift in the market, an enabling program on the web that is a useful tool for A&R, PR, labels, fans and

radio professionals alike. If physical sales are weakening, it's merely a sign that the market wants to consume its music in a more flexible way: hands up if you own an iPod, chaps.[86]

And to deal with this briefly, let's check out a coupla stories that relate to MySpace in the sense that they illustrate the potential power of peer-group networking and the huge sway that word of mouth now holds...

Jac Codi Baw[87]

Nizlopi are a duo from Warwickshire with a natty line in poppy-personal ditties. In June 2005 they released a particularly silly, but serious, ditty all about JCBs, dyslexia and bullying, cunningly titled 'The JCB Song'. It stiffed at Number 160 in the UK charts.

But then something started happening. The duo's track, complete with charming animated video, was made available for streaming from their website, jcbsong.com. People started downloading it and emailing it to each other. 'The JCB Song' video began to be shared by disparate characters all over the world, one of whom was Joe Mott of the *Daily Star*.

"It was initially in an email from someone who said 'Check out this link, it's really good'," recalls Mott, "and I rarely do that cause nine times out of ten it's just some shite program that says 'you're a twat' then you have to reboot your computer! But it was just great! It was at the time when it was becoming clear that the net was not just a novelty, it was becoming clear that it was becoming a *big* thing."

And so Joe Mott wrote about Nizlopi in his influential 'Hot' column. The internet groundswell had crossed over into the popular press. Bingo.

"I'm not saying its success was just because of me because it went to other people as well," continues Mott, "but within a week of me getting that video, a hell of a lot of people, who I wasn't necessarily immediately connected with, were talking about it, had heard it, were whistling it. It became clear that it was something that you've got to get on the back of. And I think it's the kind of thing that if you hadn't had the internet behind it, and you hadn't seen it, it would never have worked."

"Because the cartoon video – while it's good, put it on the telly and people will flick over: 'What? This Is

Rubbish! Start of the song, man with a guitar singing silly stuff?' You wouldn't give it the time of day. But because it went round to people in the offices, during the day, they might be a bit bored, they click on it and give it the time. Cause they want to get away from their work anyway. And that gives you the time to realise it's a good song, a good video, and to ping it on to someone else. Which is something that I don't think you can buy. If you could, then all the labels would be doing it, wouldn't they?"

The track was re-released in December 2005, but this time it reached Number One in the UK charts; the viral nature of its take-up was purely down to file-sharing, and interestingly it showed that if the market was on board with something they genuinely liked, they would *still pay for the physical product.*

Because people like to talk. And people like to discover. And people like to be sold *to.*

How To Get To Number One Without Selling Any Records

The UK charts are still somewhat in a state of flux, but the new wave of digital delivery has impacted heavily on their inclusion rules. After a few months of bands releasing tiny circulations of physical singles in order that their downloaded tracks would become chart eligible, the rules changed again to allow songs to chart purely on download sales. The first track to reach Number One on downloads alone was 'Crazy' by Gnarls Barkley.

"It was very simple really," begins Korda Marshall, head of Gnarls' record label, Warners. "There was a huge buzz on the record; they were late delivering the record; we kept putting the release date of the single back and back; we put it on iTunes, the uptake was enormous, it grew weekly; and when we decided to release the record the song went to Number One before we'd released the physical record. So it was indeed the first Number One record purely on download sales in isolation."

"What happened was that it was one of those classic situations where the story in itself became the story. So we realised very quickly that we could get on the news, and get a big press piece and get a whole thing about the album coming out and everything else by doing this. It gives a focal point in other media ports that we weren't able to do traditionally by just having a Number One record. So I'd like to sit here and say it was all part of the masterplan, and it was to an extent, but we rode the wave and we managed to surf it and break it at the right

time, because the single release, the digital release, the physical release and the video release were all controlled to the point where we could make it into a story."

Sam Sparrow, head of digital at Warners, takes up the baton.

"From a digital department point of view," she says, "we were thinking, 'When is this gonna happen? How is this gonna happen? Is it gonna happen?' And then obviously we had this opportunity with Gnarls, so we went for it. And like Korda said, it helped itself, really, by the story building and people saying that it might happen. What's interesting is that it hasn't happened since. No-one's gone to Number One since on downloads only, so it does have to be a very big single."

"It was more to do with the single and the time-frame and the way it was done," concludes Marshall.

"More than it was to do with the chart formulae or rules. And also this is Gnarls Barkley, I mean, it's Danger Mouse the producer; they're very technology-aware, they're very digitally-aware, they're very twenty-first century cutting-edge, so we had the support of an artist who understood what we were talking about and was prepared to gamble with us, who believed in the idea ... and we believed in them enough to make it happen. And they believed in us enough to take the risk – and it worked."

In other words, Gnarls Barkley already had credibility[88]: the record would have climbed the charts regardless of the delivery format. Because people like to listen to music, and if they like the music they will buy it.

As you were.

But 'New' Is Not The Same As 'Good'
And if you don't get that fundamental blimmin' concept I'm not going to bother talking to you anymore.

Credible Business Models Are Possible, Y'Know
Well, here it is: MySpace is a social networking site and there is money to be made from an audience and userbase of any reasonable size. Amazon.com and iTunes are testament to that. Contemporary business models must adhere, then, to the underlying issue which is that peer group credibility is the key to sustainable income streams. One of the most successful online marketplaces and gathering grounds for kids who want to be sold *to* is

Loserkids.com,[89] the UK version of which employs Lucy Hughes. They also, of course, have a massive and active presence on MySpace.

We Are All Losers

"Loserkids only went live in July 2005," Lucy says. "We started the Loserkids MySpace page in September or October 2005. It started off just being a page where we'd add people and that was it, pretty much. But I've been working on it, and now I've got an assistant to help with online marketing and there's a lot of added content – the competitions, the new products. And we check through all our friends' birthdays and we'll say happy birthday to them and stuff. MySpace is a really important thing for us – all of our big peaks, sales-wise, are around the time of our weekly newsletter. One thing that's really interesting is what happens when we put on a really new, exclusive product – I'll give you an example, we've just got some new Macbeth shoes, that no other shop has got at the moment, we've got them in a couple of months early because we distribute them. We put them online and there was no effect because there was no increased traffic to the Loserkids UK site, but we posted a bulletin on MySpace and within about an hour we'd had six orders for the new shoes. So it is that instant. And I laugh cause we post stuff up during the day at two o'clock in the afternoon when I'd think the kids, the people buying stuff from our site, would be at school! ... but they'll see something on MySpace and they'll buy it, straight away. There is a big peak from 4pm

onwards, but still if we do post something people will still notice it during the school hours – which I think is quite funny."

The main Loserkids website is an online shop, a newsletter, a forum, and a swirling party of registered subscribers. These are people who identify with the lifestyle that Loserkids offers, a social network based firmly around music.

"We're not cold-calling anyone," continues Lucy. "We have over thirty thousand kids on our mailing list, which is a lot because other companies don't go out there to gigs and stand there with a clipboard asking people to sign up to the mailing list. The way they get their database is just returning customers. But we physically go out and chat to kids and then we get their email address and we write to them. We have a weekly newsletter which is really successful for us. We try and keep it chatty, so rather than just saying: 'Buy this; this T-shirt goes nicely with this pair of jeans,' we're a lot more chatty. We're saying what gigs we're going to this week and what albums we're listening to in the office. We've just started a thing where people from bands give us their top five 'whatever', and we're putting that in the newsletter. So again it's something for the kids to read, rather than just seeing a bit of marketing that is obviously marketing, which they then forget about. We want the newsletter to be something that people expect, and look forward to, and read, and remember – and maybe even send it to one of their friends."

This new way of generating income through direct communication between the brand and the consumer[90] (or the band and the fan) is one of the key elements in the success of Loserkids and sites like it; it works, says Hughes, because rather than being a faceless multi-national corporation pushing 'cool goods' at a disinterested teenager, there is a real-world direct contact and respect involved.

"Because we do all our marketing, really, to do with music and extreme sports, we're out there at events," concludes the lass who was only just on time for our interview cause she was busy elsewhere, trying on the new range of clothes for the 2007 market. "And the music that we're aiming at, started off when we were younger – doing fanzines and DIY shows and stuff like that; and that's what we're trying to do with the website as well. It is a company and kinda corporate, that you can go to this website and buy stuff. But we still see ourselves as doing it our way, and keeping it friendly to the kids. If you compare us to some of the other websites out there, we're a lot more friendly. We have people on MySpace literally all day, every day, chatting to kids. If someone emails us, we won't just reply to it, we'll chat to them. They're asking us questions about the site, but eventually we have regular customers who'll just sit there chatting to us all day, which is ideal, because they're loyal to us; it's quite time consuming for us but we enjoy it. As well as all the online stuff, because we go to events such as festivals they can put a face to the name; they can come and chat to us. Nine times out of ten they'll come up and ask, 'Is Lucy here?' And I say, 'Yeah, that's me!' But they expect it to be somebody in the background. We're not: we're right there doing stuff ourselves all the time. We're at gigs, we'll sponsor tours, we'll put people out on tour, hand out flyers and wristbands. We do the street teaming thing, but it's paid employees going to the gigs who are enjoying it, because we want to be there anyway! We just take along some promo stuff to do at the same time."

Building networks; building credibility; building friends.

Who want to be sold *to*.

I Think This Man Has Hit The Nail On The Head Here So I'm Going To Shut Up And Let Him Talk To You Instead

"The thing that the internet has done," says Stuart Knight, co-founder of the websites X-Taster and X-360, "is democratised the relationship between the music industry and the marketplace. And it's also involved the marketplace in the process. In the past, the music industry ignored the marketplace and set its stall out: you basically bought what they put in the shops. That's how it worked: 'there's a new band, we're going to advertise it here, it's going to go on Radio One and *Top Of The Pops*, and this is what you will like.'"

"The marketplace has now changed, because you can access music without having to rely on the music industry to provide it for you. This has opened up the game immensely. It reminds me a lot of the mid-Seventies, with punk rock and the birth of the independent record company, when Stiff, and Rough Trade, and all these labels sprung up out of nowhere, with music aficionados signing punk bands, because before that it was just major record companies."

"You had labels like Phillips and Pye who would sign these bands – and they've all gone. They were killed off by the rise of the indie label. And that's very much what we're seeing now, that there's an area within the internet that allows for independent music to flourish without being reliant on a traditional model; and that's what's exciting. The other thing, of course, is that it's a two-way street; it's not an old-fashioned, late Seventies thing where you went and bought something physically – there's an interaction between the artist and (the fan). You click on the artist's page, and you've got a direct line to the artist. It's not like walking into HMV and they give you the band's phone number: you can send an email, you can download the tour dates, and you can join their street team. You can do a whole host of other things. And it's the first time we've ever been that close. Now you go to a gig and you can do meet 'n' greets, the band sign things. The citadel that the music industry sat behind is not the same anymore, and I think the majors are fighting a kind of rearguard action to protect that kind of relationship. And they're gonna fail."

"'The birth of the 7' came from that era, and this is the birth of the download. And the music industry has been really slow to react; it's only been the last two or three years. People have wanted to buy music in this format for the last ten years, and you have to remember, in an Orwellian way, that the major music machine has changed its language to suit the times. And it wasn't very long ago that people were suing the marketplace, or threatening to lock up Shawn Fanning who started Napster. Downloads were tantamount to treason! You know, you were starving bands by downloading their music, and it was a terrible kneejerk reaction. Suing the marketplace or buying them. Sue them or buy them! And now, of course, it's: 'We should absorb this technology and this is what the marketplace wants; we should be coming up with our own solutions.' What other industry in the world sues its own marketplace? Or sticks its fingers in its ears and goes, 'Lalalalala don't wanna know, don't wanna know'? That's how arrogant the industry was; it's plain to see, like the nose on your face, that a lot of executives arrogantly wouldn't even listen to their own marketplace, and that is appalling."

More Knight Fever From The Man Himself

"X-taster and our sister company, 360-x.com – which is an urban interface – started about three and a half years ago after myself and my business partner, Nick Dryden, spent some time in America and – in our previous music industry incarnations – looked at the way that music was being sold to lifestyle groups defined by music genre. For example, rock kids were being sold music by bands like Slipknot and Linkin Park who went on to sell millions and millions of albums, through non-traditional means, because they were being denied access to mainstream radio. Radio was playing HipHop in the heyday of HipHop, so rock music, particularly those bands, was being denied to a large extent. So it was all about word of mouth, and buzz, and online, that whole thing. I really thought this was fantastic and wanted to bring it back not just to the UK but to Europe."

"We came back to our lives and jobs – I ran International Recordings at the Ministry Of Sound, Nick was working within a special department in BBH, the advertising agency. The time came when we were free of our jobs and we certainly had the opportunity to do something else. So we said, 'We've always wanted to do this.' There was a paradigm shift in the way that the internet was being perceived anyway: the dot.com bubble had happened; Google was growing; and things were just starting to take shape a little bit more."

"We felt it was a really good time to get into it, so we set up in Nick's warehouse space in north London and we started to build a music community. We first started with an Excel spreadsheet and a lot of email addresses, and we populated message boards and all the rest of it. And we built up a database of people who wanted to get involved in promoting bands in a hands-on way, in exchange for getting the opportunity to actually meet the bands, or money-can't-buy incentives. We built up from there. We developed a piece of proprietary software that manages all the communications with our database. We have a core database now of around forty thousand people across the UK, who are active in promoting our bands and lifestyle campaigns, and a wider database of about a million. We get about half a million unique visitors to our website a month, probably around fifteen thousand a day, which is about enough to fill Earls Court! So we have these tastemakers and early adopters interacting with us on a daily basis in quite big numbers; we send them information about artists and bands, films, games, books: things that fit into that kind of lifestyle space."

"Because media and the interaction between social groups is so refined and confined to three basic food groups – print, radio and TV – and because the means of production, if you like, was controlled by a very small minority of people, the content of those outlets was dictated to and controlled. I don't mean in a cynical, dystopian way, what I mean is that the little man lost his voice. You'd be confined to letters to the editor. Or 'Points of View'. And what the fuck is that?! Whereas today I went to the BBC website, which is the default page in my browser, and they had an article about CBGBs in New York shutting down. And they ask for your opinions and memories. I remember managing a band – we played there in the mid-nineties, I'm a huge Ramones fan, and I remember being there and going, 'My band's playing here, it's like a dream come true.' I felt like a tile in a very big mosaic. I was reading everyone else's memories and it was just really fucking interesting, you know? All these people from all over the world who had come together in this little area to talk about their experiences. It's a fantastic example of just how uniting it can be."

"At the end of the day, MySpace and all the other similar sites are going to develop into other things over the next five or ten years and we don't know where we're going to end up. It's a bit like the Wild West; at the moment you've got the cattle barons duking it out over the ownership of the real estate. That's what you're witnessing. But you have to remember that the success of MySpace and the success of Youtube is reliant on the

marketplace – not on those companies. It's the market that populates them; it's the market that gives them their value. The thing that's trumpeted about Youtube is that a hundred million people look at it every week. Yeah, well, if something else came along, watch how quickly those hundred million desert it."

Gootube

Ah, yeah, kinda forgot about Youtube. Google bought it for loads of money. The end. This is a book about social networking sites, not Youtube. If you want to read about Youtube, go and write a book. About Youtube. You could call it *Whose Tube Is It Anyway?* Something like that. Have fun.

Rupert [91] Bares His Teeth And Puts His Money Where His Mouth Is[92]

"I wanted Murdoch to buy Manchester United. I was the only United fan who wanted Murdoch to buy United, I couldn't believe it when the (other fans) were whinging

135

and whining. And then they got the Glaziers buying us, with debt. The fans got everything they fucking deserved, the arseholes." – Anthony H. Wilson[93]

Actually, News Corporation bought MySpace's parent company, Intermix, midway through the last chapter, but I swerved it cause it'd just have confused matters. Given that, arguably, the basis of the initial success and immense uptake of MySpace can be traced back to its perceived 'underground' credibility, Murdoch's[94] purchase in 2005 certainly provoked heated debate.

The central concern was that here was a phenomenon that had been built on the spirit of the internet and, until now, had been apparently uninvolved in the corporate world. Now, one of the most powerful media magnets in the universe owned it, raising a very simple question: how would this affect MySpace? "I'll tell you another thing that was very interesting," says Billy Bragg and, as ever with that chap, he does offer some very interesting food for thought, "Obviously the question people were asking was [what were] Murdoch's plans for MySpace? Was he going to move it from being a community to some form of hybrid between a record company and a radio station and whatever else? So there was all that bubbling underneath, people were wondering about all of that."

People still are, to an extent: News Corporation's purchase of the site raised i-Brows all over the place.[95]

But what exactly had they bought? If the site is defined by its users, then the content is too.

NME editor Conor McNicholas's view is that, "They've bought a whole load of servers, a brand name, some good brains, and a kind of marketing footprint, which is only as relevant and worthwhile as long as it's actually there. And the job now – like any media company – is to make sure that they actually keep them there, and stay one step ahead of the consumers to make sure that they've actually got what the consumers want. It's a tough job – but it's the same thing that we all do."

"When you own a newspaper, you own bricks and mortar," agrees X-Taster firebrand Stuart Knight, "and you own a big workforce, and you own all these assets. But if you examine what you own with MySpace, what do you own? A domain name, and some software, and it [could perhaps] be very easy to replicate that; but you don't own the people that give it the value, do you? You don't own the real value, which is the people who populate it. If everyone posted their music on another site, then what would you have?"

"To be honest with you, as much as Rupert Murdoch gets a bad time for whatever reason, he's a fairly shrewd businessman," says *NME*.com editor Ben Perreau. "I very much doubt that he's made a bad decision with MySpace. I very much doubt if he's going to let it fall over and go wrong. It'll be interesting to see how they engage with it, cause his buy-up came only six months after we heard related stories like how *The Sun* was not going to publish any of their news on the website; it was going to make everyone read the paper. *The Sun* still has quite a conservative policy on how it publishes on the web." You can see their point, to a degree. Millions of people can receive their news from millions of sources; if you make it that easy to join a mailing list, then where is the incentive to hand over the few pence for a hard copy?

"I guess that, at the very least," continues Ben, "it will be an amazing way for [Murdoch] to pro-actively get in touch with people about new Fox programming, Sky stuff, features he's got on people that are involved with the MySpace network. Some of the stuff that's been going down with the Borat film has been well promoted through MySpace, for example."

One of the worries for MySpace users may be that, when they signed up for a MySpace account, it had a mischievous, anarchic feel to it. Will the involvement of a huge corporation dent that underground vibe?

Sean Adams runs Drowned In Sound Records, one of the most exciting indie labels to have risen over the last few years. As site founder of the incredibly popular online music magazine, drownedinsound.com, he knows a thing or two about digital media. But he does not see the future as bright for MySpace.[96]

"I think MySpace lost whatever it could have been long before Murdoch got involved," he says sadly. "With all that investment they should have improved it so much, but it's still full of [issues]. I think it's essentially a massive brand and they've already started with adverts ... there's a huge social responsibility with something that large which allows people to interact."

As always, the financiers and money men will be under close scrutiny from the users/consumers. There are plenty of examples where corporate intervention has destroyed a product's appeal, but likewise post-Millennial business giants are not so blinkered that they will ride rough-shod over an investment of that scale. They are, after all, looking for a return. [(97)]

"As people were talking about taking it over," says Sammy Andrews, "it was losing the push cause people loved it at the start. It was this little community and as it's grown it's got fantastic but the users themselves don't like the fact it's lost its appeal for the underground. There was a revolt on MySpace when Fox took it over – that was a first push and we saw more adverts coming on. Everything changed, people's views on it changed, purely because of [that] and nothing else. All of a sudden everyone's just a little bit wary – and the band features page on MySpace, everything being pushed at you took a different spin. People became aware that it's possibly being paid for now [from a marketing buget]."

"Organisations can be owned by large media companies and it makes absolutely bugger all difference," contrasts Conor McNicholas. "If you really want to trace it up, *NME* is part of the biggest media company on the planet, Time Warner. But you wouldn't know it, and frankly we, the *NME* staff, wouldn't know it; we're so minuscule compared to what they do and frankly our independence is our greatest strength, and I think they (News Corp) know that about MySpace. So I think, content-wise, that's not a problem."

"But then again, they don't generate any content anyway, do they? It's user-generated content. Their biggest worry is something that's not really my area, but it is, 'how do they relate to Google and Youtube – and what does all that stuff mean for the future?' There's so much Youtube stuff embedded into MySpace pages that they have to be able to work together; the people [involved in this] copyrighted [material] are the likes of Viacom, News International and Time Warner – somebody's going to have to sort [it all out] at some point and MySpace is gonna have to work out what their role is in the middle of the whole thing."

Which brings us nattily onto this bit here, which you'd already be reading if this sentence wasn't quite so stretched-out and pointless as it is in danger of becoming, because I'm hung-over and my fingers and brain appear to be moving of their own accord at the moment; I'm sorry about that, but it's been a strange and wonderful time of late and I think I'm losing the last of whatever remaining piece of mind I once allowed to fight and flay with freedom and occasional love when I had enough money to buy some.

Home Taping Is Killing Music: Copyright Conundra And Impending Digital Disasters

"The amount of money that [can be made] off of MySpace," says Billy Bragg, "[is] off the back of free content. So one question then arises as to whether or not there should be some form of royalty paid to people who put material on MySpace, cause we're providing a service. If you have your records played on commercial radio and the BBC, you get paid a royalty because you're bringing listeners in. Well, the content that appears on MySpace is bringing a particularly difficult-to-reach age group together, which allows [Myspace] to get very high advertising rates to show them adverts." It's one hypothesis.

"I think we're at a paradigm shift in the industry: you no longer need to sign your entire catalogue away to a label for life of copyright. You can licence: five years, ten years or whatever. And I'd really like people to appreciate that before they come in. I'm alright because I've got a publishing deal and a record label deal, and I don't know for sure but I bet those deals could override the Terms and Conditions of MySpace. I don't know; I'm assuming that."

The point has to be made, however, that MySpace were never attempting to sneak ownership of anyone's rights or copyright, it was, as discussed, a process of not having to *pay out* for the material posted. Their clarification of those Terms and Conditions may hopefully be a watershed moment for such material on the web.

Billy feels that the success of MySpace and the subsequent 'ownership' concerns presents an ideal chance to start again. "I believe there should be an industry standard for this kind of thing, under which the sites operate. Where people are providing originated content. A double-edged proprietary rights clause, in which artists own the right to original material but also undertake not to use other people's material. The other part of the proprietary clause is that 'you represent and warrant that you own the content posted by you, and you have the right to grant us this licence.' Which I think is fair. So the proprietary rights issue becomes double-edged. You've got a cast iron defence for your own originally created content, but you're also offering the site that you're posting on indemnity that you're not posting stuff that's not original material. I think that's only fair; it doesn't need to be a one- way street, but it does need an industry standard."

"The way we used to think of copyright is going to have to change, but ownership of intellectual property rights is a big-handled word; the right to exploit material that you've created. Who owns that right? Should that right be my pension or should it be the pension of someone faceless in a multinational corporation? That's what's at stake for me; it's always been at stake for me and my records. I've always had to have that conversation with my record company: 'These are my rights, and they must revert to me.' Those issues, of reversion and ownership, although perhaps not germane to what's happening on MySpace, the MySpace paradigm gives us a real opportunity not only to air this issue but to improve the lot of artists."

"Nobody knows what the music industry will look like in ten or fifteen years time, but I can assure you there'll be plenty of people making music. That's absolutely guaranteed, so it would be really good if we could use this time of change to strengthen both the rights of the originator and also the relationship and distance between the artist and their audience – which has always been kept [distant] by physical manufacture and distribution; when you made a record, if you wanted it to be in shops in New York, Liverpool or Australia, you had to go with a big label. And not only did they have to make the records and carry them to these places, they also had to be big enough to make sure that people paid them. Now, with digital distribution, none of that is necessary, our hand as artists is strengthened. I think that the MySpace phenomenon has just shifted the sand beneath the feet of the majors, and they're still working out how the fucking hell to respond. Meanwhile, people are carrying on making good music and perhaps are more inclined to do so now that they know that they don't have to tread that difficult road."

"It's made the major labels a lot less precious about the 'value' of their content," says Sean Adams. "But at the same time made it so that the barriers have dropped so low they've completely devalued their product and artistry and I'm not sure how they ever expect to monetise a culture so used to listening to music for free all day long. I don't understand how the old precedents – radio led us to having publishing and high video royalties from MTV2, etc – could have slipped away."

"The thing about MySpace," according to Stuart Knight, "is that it's too indiscriminate. It's just a big website. It's like a huge warehouse full of music. How do you know which part of the warehouse has got what you're looking for? You walk in there, you could be walking around it for days trying to find what you want – unless someone gives you a signpost. And who's going to give you the signpost? If you said to me, 'Hey Stuart, it's Joe, there's this amazing new band, Joe And The Bastards, go and check them out, it's www.MySpace.com/joeandthebs', you've given me a signpost. That's the problem with it. There's a lot of myth associated with MySpace: 'This band's getting five million streams on MySpace!' Well? What does that mean? You know, and how is that gonna transfer into the sales of records? There's a whole load of questions about it."

"I think the financial value has transferred," says Korda Marshall. "Kids are putting an enormous amount of value in going to see bands live; there is a very large value attached to the music. Whether it's free or not it's still very valuable to them culturally and socially, playground-wise, and listening-wise, and knowing-what's-happening-wise. So there's still an inherent value in it in a marketing sense or a promotional sense – but there's less of a value in a payment sense. But I think the models will 'sophisticate' themselves, like the Napster one did, it was free initially, radio was free initially then it started advertising; a lot of industries start free and then develop a price structure formula. That'll happen with digital music on the web as it has happened with many other industries."

"It's an exciting format, an exciting new trend: the jury's out; I still have a perception that they've built their business on other people's copyrights and that ultimately will come to an end, but it's exciting and it's challenging – and it means that [sometimes with Youtube and sites like it] I have to go out and see less gigs because I can just watch it all on the computer at home! It's challenging: we need to embrace the future and march into it rather than do what the traditional record business has done for the last ten years and run away from it and try and sue everyone."

Dance Music Is Alive And Well, Thank You Very Much, Stop Going On About Its Demise Please

Gavin Herlihy is the Features Editor of Europe's biggest dance music Magazine, *Mixmag*. He's also a techno-freak, to the point that he *doesn't even own a telly!* Which is worrying, cause the only other person I know who doesn't own a television spends all his time *playing the piano, and reading books, and learning things, and creating art!* Which quite frankly is completely weirdo behaviour that we thought we'd stamped out years ago.

"It's obviously an important resource in the DJs' and artists' repertoire of tools that they use to reach their audience," says Herlihy. "What I find quite interesting is that DJs are often easier to contact via MySpace than they are through a PR, or through their own email.

Some of them seem to have taken to MySpace very readily, and you can always spot them. Some guys' sites are very PR [created]; the blurb at the top says 'This is the official page for blah blah blah', the biog is written by someone else rather than their own personalised thing. But then there are people like Erol Alkan, for instance, who definitely furthers his name and his career by the fact that he's a very approachable guy on MySpace. You could probably strike up a conversation with him or approach him about something that he's doing, as a fan, and get a response from him."

But for the dance music fraternity, the community-building side of MySpace is utilised very efficiently too. It's been perfect in keeping in contact with new friends and old. We've all done it; spending all night with your arms round strangers, half-naked and sweaty in random Northern clubs that are dressed up like a Victorian boudoir, and vowing tearily and wearily to stay in touch as the sun comes up. But then you lose their numbers along with your short-term memory. And then you lose their numbers ... oh.

"I think the other important thing," continues Gavin, "is that its greatest impact is just on people themselves. How people socialise and continue friendships after a club, and how promoters make use of that. In my case, I've got so many really, really good friends who don't actually live in my home town, but to all intents and purposes they might as well do because I'm constantly chatting to them on MySpace, we're

looking at pictures of what we were up to on the weekend, what clubs we've been to, messaging each other during work."

Dance music, much in line with the reasons Dave Bamforth set up Faceparty in the first instance, has always had that sense of closeness about it; uniquely, there's a wider openness at work, which makes the concept of a community a very different one to those which gather round, and are even mobilised by, specific bands.

"It probably has more of an effect in dance music in that sort of sense than it has in the indie scene," agrees Gavin, "cause the indie scene is ruthless in the sense that there's lots of bands campaigning for fans and really working their MySpace marketing to the bone. Dance music on MySpace isn't so much about that; it's more about people. It's more about social groups, so it's kind of empowering the punters really. The artists and the DJs definitely get something out of it, but not to the same extent as the people."

"It's been a vital way for communities of people who met in clubs to continue their friendship or interaction during the week," he muses. "Defying geographical boundaries. For instance, I was in Mexico City last week on a job[98] and met lots of people who are mutual friends of mine through travelling around, and MySpace, and now we're firm buddies and send each other messages every day which would never have been possible before. From a club promoter's perspective this is amazing because the thing about dance music, since the demise of the superclub, is that club culture has become more about crowds of people again – and not name DJs. It's become more about friendships that people make on dancefloors, and the little social bonds they make that make them want to come back to a club. MySpace is such an important part of that now that most promoters don't bother with traditional websites anymore. They just opt for a MySpace page which is easier to set up and far more effective in being able to message their dancefloor, and for their dancefloor to keep in contact with each other in leaving each other messages, becoming friends and all that kind of thing."

So the media really should have been drawing parallels between dance music and MySpace, rather than trying to bolt together Monkeys and MySpace, but, hey, according to sections of the popular press, dance is dead, right?[(09)] Ha. Regardless, the dance scene turns up some surprising people living in MySpace, too.

"It's really weird, you get random individuals there like Keith Chegwin for instance," laughs the man with no television. "He absolutely loves MySpace. Up North, 'Cheggers' or 'Keith Chegwin' is slang for Ketamine. All these club kids have been messaging him. He, of course, thinks it's amazing that suddenly all these cool young club kids think he's really interesting and want to get in touch with him and be his friend."

Oops.

Busted!

Sorry chaps, just pretend you haven't read that last bit because y'know, my short-term memory ain't so good these days and neither is my short-term memory.

Er, okay. But, y'know, erm, why haven't you got a telly Gavin? Isn't that a bit... y'know?

"The days of TV being the most important piece of technology in your life are going to be over," he responds. "So I don't have a TV at home; I have an internet connection – I could get all my entertainment purely out of MySpace and Youtube and news websites if need be. I think that's a trend that's going to increase because people are more likely to be entertained by communicating again and speaking to each other and socialising rather than watching something on a TV screen. There'll always be a place for that but the balance of interests will shift toward MySpace and stuff in the future."

Very intriguing... maybe it's time to go crusading again, then.

The Web 2.0 Myth

"The power is with the market. It's uncontrollable. The thing is, with commerce and capitalism at the moment there's this lie that there's a free market. There isn't. It's a controlled market. If it was a free market we wouldn't be subsidising fishermen and farmers. We wouldn't be paying BMW to keep the factories open. Everyone would be at the mercy of market forces, and if they're making a loss, they're making a loss. You're not Railtrack, we're not paying dividends... you're not making a bet on a horse, and demanding your winnings if it comes in fifth. That's what big business is all about these days; 'Oh well, we'll move our factories to India'. Well, fucking move them to India then! It's supposed to be market forces. Somebody explain to me that if we've got a free market why don't we live or die by the market forces? It's protectionism: it's like a racket. And what I think the internet potentially does offer is, 'I'm sorry, but you can't (control this), it's too free and open, and it's global.' So what's gonna happen when the marketplace turns round, en masse, and says, 'Well, sod you!'? Your value is just gonna fall away." – Stuart Knight, X-Taster[100]

Web 2.0 is – according to some vague techno-utopian, *Guardian*-reading, woolly-jumpered, folk fans I just completely made up then vacuously stereotyped – some kind of free, open, idealistic new digital world where programs exist only to allow its users to generate their own content. A network within which anyone can post whatever they like, listen to what they like and watch whatever they like – whenever they like. A pull rather than a push; user-generated content and on-demand anti-scheduled time-shifted content.[101] It all sounds very familiar doesn't it? And in a sense, that's accurate enough; in another sense, it brings with it one whole bunch of other questions, which are fundamentally down to monetisation of that content, as well the credibility of the cues you choose to take.

"People think they need traditional media less," says Mark Sutherland, "whereas in a weird way perhaps they need it more than ever *because* there is all this information out there. In fact, you would think the filter devices that good publications provide would be more useful than ever. But I think there has been a kind of perception change in everything really. Perhaps people are less worried about whether something is brilliant before they become interested in it. 'I'll just download this track, it's free, there's not really any investment in it, just listen to it and if I like it, I like it. I don't need somebody telling me that I ought to go and seek it out.'"

"I wouldn't say it's redundant, because I think good critics and good publications can still provide a really important service – and a lot of what we do here at *Billboard* is precisely that; making sense of these things for our readership – but equally I think there are people out there who aren't so fussed about an *NME* recommendation as they would have been five years ago."

"Our role is much more of a filter and an arbitrator now," says *NME* editor Conor McNicholas. "There's loads of stuff out there, but the thing about MySpace is that it's basically just an enormous, fuck-off database and you can access all of that content really quickly, so our role is to go 'actually *this* is the thing that you really ought to be looking at, because whether they've got 100,000 friends or not, *this* is the best thing. And also *that* thing that people are going on about, *that's* actually not very good; *this* thing that people are going on about –

yes, *this* is the real deal. And we're gonna take it to another level, we're gonna embrace your endorsement, and we're gonna put them on the cover, or give them a feature, or whatever.'"

Cultural value, rather than financial.

"It's really quite fundamentally changed our role," he concedes. "Historically, bands would tour their arse off, try and get noticed by an A&R guy, would sign a record deal which was the Big Win, and then somebody at a record company would tell *NME* about this band – and for most people in the world, most music fans in a band, certainly in our area, a group didn't exist until *NME* talked about them. There was no other way of finding out. Nowadays, signing a record deal is almost the end of the process, which is what record companies are finding so difficult. What we don't do is kind of say 'there's this new band that everybody's going on about' because everybody's going on about shitloads of new bands, all the time."

"But it does change the way that we talk about music; it's much more of a filter now, rather than just mining for gems and holding them up."

And the Arctic Monkeys weren't on the cover of that magazine until *after* they'd had a Number One record. The world has changed, and insanely so. The power may be in filtered peer group recommendation, but indications suggest that MySpace and Google have based a large chunk of their income on targeted advertising at the moment; Google search itself is based on directing the user to other people's content, and MySpace, arguably, does the same. But not everybody has the talent or nous to put up interesting stuff…

(Jeremy Beadle Is To Blame

Remember those home video clip shows that were seemingly commissioned by TV guys in cahoots with the major breweries, that made you want to scream in pain at the scorched skies and run down to your local pub a little bit earlier than you'd originally planned every Saturday night? User-generated content, y'see. But after you've seen four videos of cats looking a little bit like Hitler, and seven babies falling asleep in their mushy bowls of radioactive-hued alphabetti spaghetti, it gets a bit fucking tiresome.)

…so naughty people started to whack up copyright content of people who were genuinely talented. Bad and naughty, and wholly unworkable because Home Taping Is Killing Music, remember? In the autumn of 2006, MySpace announced two major collaborative deals. Firstly, they would be using Gracenote software to crack down on the unauthorized use of copyright content – a program that looks at the 'musical fingerprint' of tracks and compares it with songs already in its database. If it matches, and the user who posted it is not the copyright owner, the track will be taken down and offending profiles deleted from the system. Fair play.

Secondly, MySpace teamed up with Snocap, a software which will enable artists to set up their own

download shops to sell tracks through their MySpace page. Snocap software was invented and programmed by Shawn Fanning.[102]

MySpace Sponsor Cool Stages At Festivals And Have A Record Label Too

"They've done a really good job at sitting themselves there alongside music – their brand is very much part of the puzzle wherever you look; whether it's on tour, at festivals... and that's certainly increasing. They're doing these secret MySpace shows now, there's a lot of potential there with what they can do with that content, cause they're now owning exclusive content. If they have a show where, for example, My Chemical Romance play, then [if] they own that content, that video footage or that audio footage, that's when you can start looking at monetising it. Then you can offer the subscription thing where if you pay a premium you have access to extra material or something like that."

- Stuart Clarke, *Music Week*

Perhaps generating and exploiting exclusive content – such as the streaming of Fox shows on MySpace and the comedy, film collaborations and exclusive webcasts of live bands – is indeed the way forward. But that's not exactly this Web 2.0 utopia we keep hearing about, now is it?

"I don't know about MySpace," says Serena Wilson, "but there's going to be some money changing hands soon; charging for music seems inevitable and working alongside the major labels – there's going to be collaborations, as there are with all those major companies – mergers. But what the future looks like for music online – nobody knows, which is exciting. But it's definitely a test of how resilient the current state of the music industry is. Coming up with new media is really pushing them to the limit."

"The future – I don't know. I'd love to know; I feel it's still unclear what a successful model for selling music online will look like. One thing is certain: the new vision of music is open, democratic, cheap or free."

But maybe the future is already here. And, hey, guess what? It's exactly the same as the past was.

"I think it's been a natural, organic thing," says Jamie Nelson, "and obviously if you look at the broader internet element of it, historically that was just a means of communication for people and naturally it becomes more commercial. Inevitably that's probably what will happen with all of these mediums. That's naturally the way that they progress. In the long term, no doubt there will be other forms of MySpace that crop up, and other ways of communicating – more things like Youtube – there'll be more of these kind of things coming through over the coming years, that are a progression on what this is. It's just the natural evolution that we have on the web. But ultimately all these things are based around the same thing – from an A&R and music perspective – which is that people with great talent and exciting ideas and great songs will find their way through, and all of these things around them will just become the forum for them to get their music and their talent heard."

"I think we're at a stage now," muses Joe Mott, "where we've got this new thing, and we've nearly worked out how to use it but we're not there yet. We haven't let go of the old, and we haven't fully grasped the new, and as soon as we do it'll get catalysed on and we'll have to move on again."

Because the web never stands still, and because people like to talk.

The Money Is Already In The System

Korda Marshall: "It's already been monetised; it's just that the money's not coming to the people who are creating the art. The telecoms companies are making a fortune out of it. It costs a lot to buy a computer and get it set up and the mouse and everything else around it, and the monthly payments for your broadband; that's not cheap music, that's not free music – that's quite expensive."

A very good point indeed. But where does that all
leave us?

ooooh

Part Six

The Future In The Words Of Those Who Are Already There

The Future According To My Favourite Austrian Ex-Ice-Dancer

"I can see myself watching TV in five years time when it's all over, and there'll be endless documentaries about the impact of MySpace on the 2000s, etc; and there'll be a 1984-stylee horrorvision on Channel Four and Channel Five. Or something like, 'In twenty years' time we will not leave our homes anymore because we only exist in cyberspace, which eventually will lead to the breakdown of humanity as we know it and we will revert to live like they thought it was cool in medieval times'. That will be the e4 version."

– Eli Fritsche, Music Promoter

Proper Convergence Is Coming, According To Sammy Andrews, Oh, And By The Way, Email Is Dead

"There's a whole generation of kids who have grown up communicating with a webcam or being creative with videos," says the Digital/Viral consultant at the forefront of her profession. "People are like that with their MySpace stuff. Hosting your videos on MySpace is great. Instant messaging is massive, and MySpace offers it. If there was something like MySpace with emails rolled into one, if your message box looked like an email, people would use it for email. Everyone I know has a MySpace page open and their email program at the same time. If there was a site, exactly the same as MySpace, which offered better communication with emails and filing systems and took over email, everyone would go there."

"There are places where (technically) MySpace falls back, but as a bare bones site, it's a sign of things to come. Kids are going to sit in their houses and watch things and terrestrial telly will go out the window. As Youtube Channels develop; generally, I think the whole user-generated thing is the future. It's here and it's only going to get bigger."[103]

"The direct sales concept; I think on the internet as a whole there's a lot of little shops that sell any object that you like, specialist shops that the internet has blossomed for. A lot of traditional smaller (real) shops have died because you can get stuff on the internet; they can import stuff, places [that feel like] a whole life community, like that Japanese site which has everything – a shop, a social network area, music – you get it all for a subscription fee, that is where I think everything is going.[104] If you subscribed it would more than triple the music industry's income."

"A lifestyle site is the future and I'm just waiting for somebody to do it properly. This is why MySpace did so well; the users got on first and the credibility grew

because it was user-generated and not forced upon people. You can't do it if you force it on people, you have to have grass roots there and that's just how it works on the internet. If the whole internet population is against you, you're out. I honestly think you're just going to be able to log on to one page where you've got email, home shopping, a list of friends, music, all in one. Youtube, Skype, all these things added into one. And TV at some point as well; you don't have to pay for any of these individual services, they're all on a computer screen."

"Teenagers in the last five years would come home," suggests Korda Marshall, from a completely different interview, physical space, and date, "And slob out on the couch and channel-hop on TV; they'd watch Scuzz, and Amp, and MTV2; they'd tune into what they wanted and skip onto the next one if they didn't [like what was on at the time]. Now they come home and they get onto MySpace. What it's doing is that it's weakened the traditional media outlets of say Radio One, or XFM, or radio generally, and it's weakened digital TV and other forms of media entertainment. Because people can discover (things) for themselves, and make their own playlists, and discover their own music rather than being fed or told what they like by national radio stations or newspapers or TV stations."

"Although there's another view," he ponders, "which says the mass common denominator is probably the worst. Just cause eighty thousand people go and see it one day doesn't mean that it's the best, or the most creative. But, again, it multi-dimensions the media so it's videos and it's other bits and bobs, and it's money shots: it's all kinds of things. It's not just a context of whether they like the song or not; what that digital content can be is many other things other than just a song."

The Future According To Alex Cameron, Who Knows Loads Of Stuff About TV On The Net[105]

"When you've got an absolutely unstoppable amount of digital media, an absolute mess of it, it's impossible to find your way around," he declares. "That's the problem with it; it's incredibly difficult. And you tend to find that the old media way is that you push things at people; whereas the new media way is that people assume that others are going to search or actively look for content; the old media world says that human beings are lazy and need things pushed at them. When you're outside a tube station, a paper is thrust into your hand; if you want to watch football matches, they're on Sky Sports; you read an advert or read something a journalist's written. Basically the information is put to you, it's pushed at you. And if you look at what MySpace does, it's very clever compared to everything on the other sites: they update you all the time; they're always pushing things at you. They're pushing event messages. When you've got new messages, new blogs and that kind of thing. They're continually pushing new notifications at you, and giving you a reason, pushing you back to the site. Or pulling you back, if you like."

"The other thing is that social networking's very natural; we've been doing it for three thousand years. There's nothing about social networking that's remotely new, and there's nothing new about user-generated content; we had *You've Been Framed* ten years ago. Everything On Demand in the world: we talk about IPTV being On Demand; people make it out, with big hype, as this massive revolution."

"It's not. We've been doing everything on demand for millennia. You go into a supermarket and you buy a loaf of bread when you want to; it's on demand. Scheduling broadcasting, from a TV perspective, is actually a very unnatural thing. So a lot of its success is not because it's a new technology, it's just automating, in some ways, electronically doing things that we do in a very natural and familiar way."

"I put a business plan together two years ago for a friend who was building a dating site. I said, 'What you need is a unified communications model – like eBay are doing, putting Skype into their web pages – you get alerts and communications via an instant messaging tool.' So the next step up for MySpace? If I were them I'd put a Voice Over IP on the instant messenger. And start allowing people to make free calls. It's just the same model. Advertising-supported models have been here for hundreds of years. You see adverts on ITV, which is a channel entirely supported by advertising."

"Websites are becoming web applications, and with the advent of IPTV, which is a medium that uses internet technology, any device that speaks IP can speak to any other. So you're getting to the point where you're getting these consolidations. Community is no longer about pages on the net – they're about other ways to integrate. Like VOIP, Skype with eBay – they've gone from being this Web 2.0 model, this whole software application, to wider communications. And that's the next step. 2D web pages are one thing, but being able to call people directly from them is an entirely different thing, on different devices."

Mobile Is King

Oh Christ, let's not get into mobile content; that is a whole other kettle of pots. But yeah, that's where the money's headed next. So if you're smart you'll track what MySpace are planning in that regard. Then you can write a book about it, called *Whose Mobile Is It Anyway?* Or maybe *My Bile Or Yours*. Have fun. I look forward to reading that too.

Last.fm And Collaborative Filtering Made Simple Through Complex Means

And this is where it starts to come together properly. Last.fm is a very viable model that acts both as a genuine peer-filtered music source and a verifiable source for actual figures as to how popular a track may or may not be. Whilst MySpace playcounts are often unreliable, and at worst open to manipulation, last.fm's are a genuine indicator. It is an impressive concept, and one that holds within it some clues as to where we may be headed, for music in practical terms, but the theory can be applied across the board too.

"Last.fm originally came together out of two projects," begins site founder Martin Stiksel. "One was a platform for unsigned artists and bands, which Felix Miller and myself had founded in about 1999/2000. It was one of these platforms where you could upload your music as a self-creating artist or band. And in a very short time we were inundated with a lot of really great music.

But we had the problem that nobody knew any of the music, or the artists' names. So we were thinking about a level way to connect people with the right music; about how you as a music fan could find music even though you might not know the name of the band or the artist. Because even Google can't help you there, if you don't know what to type in. There's no way to find anything."

"And then the second strand of thought," continues Stiksel, "that led us to last.fm was the Audioscrobbler idea, a project originally started by Richard Jones in Southampton as his final project for his computer science degree. It was looking at the scenario from a different angle: how can you find more of the music that you like? In this day and age, where there's so much choice out there, basically you need recommendations because otherwise it scares you off from exploring more, because there's just so much out there and it's not a question anymore of availability. It's very much a question of, 'How to actually find the music which is right for me, which is interesting for me.'

"So it was from a music fan's perspective, and we brought these two strands together and started working together in 2002. Essentially, these were two sides of the same coin, just looking at it from different angles. We realised that obviously the system that we developed out of this was monitoring, tracking what people were listening to; building a music profile out of that, then comparing these music profiles among each other and making intelligent predictions on what you might like as well."

"That's the collaborative filtering aspect, really, which is inspired to a certain extent by amazon.com: 'People who purchased this, also purchased that.' We have, 'People who listened to this, also listened to that. That's why you should check it out.' Arguably, our data is a lot better because currently we're getting thirty million play counts a day. So thirty million times, our people are telling us what they're listening to – this is our scrobbles – thirty million songs scrobbled a day. Arguably, this data is more valuable than just purchase information like Amazon has, because you never know with Amazon whether people actually liked the CD that they bought, or did they give it to their girlfriend as a present, or what. With last.fm, if you listen to a song fifty times in a week, it's a very, very strong value statement. And you don't need to add any rating or anything after that; it's already enough for us to make some assumptions about you and then to try to connect you with some other music that you should check out and other people that like the same music as you."

Which is a very effective cultural value indicator as well as a powerful social networking tool, and a self-perpetuating one.

"It's an ecosystem, a little one," Stiksel confirms. "The social component of keeping up with what your friends are listening to. Also there's the events system we introduced, where you can find out about where your friends are going to and which gigs they're going to. This is music information and music discovery. It brings the whole thing full cycle again – you can see who else is going to be there and maybe you might speak to them at the gig. It really brings it round to real life again. All the digital identity and things like this then

170

come full circle in the gigs. I think music is one of the strongest social glues that there is out there. There's little doubt that music is *the* community; after language and religion, I think music comes third."

I'd put it above both of 'em, meself, like. But I am in many ways a soulless and incoherent man, I guess. But you can now post your last.fm charts in your social network site of choice, too, converging things even further.

"When we started, there was no Friendster, no MySpace yet," muses the affable German. "They came along as we were doing it, and then at that moment we realised that we actually had a network in our hands – because we had profile pages and user pictures – and as soon as you have that, you're more or less a social network. And we saw that your favourite music features very strongly; it's one of these things that almost everybody has filled out in comparison to books and films. They're not so polarising; music is very, very polarising and we are offering this also as a feature for our users. You can grab your last.fm charts, your top songs, the top artists, from our website – and put it onto your blog, or onto your website, or into your MySpace profile. So a lot of people have been doing this and it's one of our main agents for growth, people eventually using one of our assets for their own web pages, for their own blogs, and things like this."

"Last.fm is trying to make this music discovery and music promotion automatic for you," reiterates Stiskel. "If you put music in there and give it a starting point with a tag, or some similar artists, then it spreads from listener to listener. Somebody listens to it, likes it, it gets passed on to other people that like similar kinds of music and if your music is really good it travels around the system automatically. Our intention was really to take the hassle out of music promotion. MySpace is like your other web page that you have to drive traffic to, for people to pay attention, whereas we have more of a push model: the radio brings you new music, music recommendation, exposes you to new music tailored to your taste without you really having to go out of your way to get all of these results."

The music industry would do well to look deeply at last.fm. This information, this user-data, this music-listening-data, is based on consumption – not assumption.

"The music industry is definitely very interested in the general music users' information that we have. And we haven't really done anything specific with the data. We're just using it for our website where it's accessible for everybody to go," concludes Stiksel, "So it's definitely extremely helpful data for a variety of applications. You could be confronted with a situation where you have two or three demos, and you don't know which one to go for – you can chuck them onto last.fm and in a short time you know which one is doing best. Or you wanna find out what the single should be of a certain release, or trying to find out what would be the best 'Best Of' compilation you're doing of a band that hasn't released anything for a while. All this information, you can garner from last.fm and therefore get a lot more information out of it."

Which is nice.

Self-Selecting Communities

"I think the people who go on MySpace know that at certain points whatever they're into is going to have bigger brands or corporations involved in it. As long as it doesn't dominate it and change how people feel about it, then it can carry on. I think what you might find is that it's getting so big that you're getting a lot of similar sites starting to take off that maybe aren't as wide, genre-wise, as MySpace. There are different sites springing up. More boutique versions of it will probably be the way forward."

– Darrin Woodford,
Independent Music Management

So rather than one, monstrous, catch-all site, perhaps niche communities will form; MySpace allows you to pick and choose your own bespoke community based round friends, films, *Playboy* models and musicians with whom you identify. But that's no different to linking to other traditional websites in your own web page. MySpace acts as another browser. An easy-to-navigate one, but it's not a *replacement* for the web – unless all the technologies make themselves intrinsically compatible, as last.fm has. "For us it was always very important to have a very clear focus to our network," agrees Martin Stiksel, "I think we'll see specialist networks emerging; last.fm could be one – a social music network which is essentially what we are. That could be one way of looking at it; specialist social networks emerging, which they already are: 'linkedin', for professional contacts, 'adultfriendfinder' which is for special interests as well, to a certain extent. Definitely around certain interests there are strong networks emerging, like the photosharing sites. I can see it fragmenting again because now MySpace is like a hold-all, just like anything that gets too big, it fragments up into small parts. I would expect it to happen to a certain extent. Like what we saw with Youtube, for example, it's a video social network, there's no doubt about that. They own social video on the net. That's my simplistic answer; it's maybe going to break up."

"The way it's playing out at the moment," adds Friends Reunited's Jon Clark, "is that the nicheness comes from the shared content; the mash-up culture where you might have your MySpace page, but you host your pictures somewhere else because it's a better service or you have more space. And I think it's using the right platform, for the right audience and the right content."

"These big brands that have exploded, continues Clark, "are good from a knowing-where-to-go point of view but they still have the challenge in that there's still an awful lot of rubbish in there. I guess one of the main benefits of social networking sites is that the scale decides what's good and what's bad. If it's not getting scale it won't get the traffic. So it's self-selecting and self-prophesising in a way I guess. I'm not sure whether the quality issues have been solved or exacerbated by these sites; it's good to have more content but there's still more

to be done by everyone in the internet community to make sense of this content and package it in a way which is meaningful and trustworthy."

"I prefer not to be on MySpace but not because of safety," offers Joshua Holmes, who runs the Christian social community, MyPraize.com. "I prefer to stay away because of the content. But, I realize that parents are concerned with their child's safety, and I can understand. I would not want my child on MySpace either; however, I think some older, more mature teens can use MySpace as a great place to witness. There are definitely concerns, and there are dangers, but you'll never get parents and users to make decisive decisions on the safety of MySpace."

"The concept behind our site was simple," explains Holmes. "There were no morally safe social networks on the internet. More specifically, there was no place for Christians to gather and not have to worry about porn or inappropriate content all over the site. After a couple weeks of playing around and debating some ideas, I started creating MyPraize.com. The main idea behind MyPraize was to create a site free of porn, foul language, suggestive poses and the threats of predators, while maintaining an atmosphere which is non-offensive to Christians and non-Christians."

You always have been able to choose your friends; [106] the only thing that's changed is that you can choose where you find them and where (and whether) you subsequently congregate.

What A Social Community Really Is

"I think as far as the internet generation goes, we will be here for a while, because once you get a taste for something it's kinda hard to go back to not having it, you know? However, as far as [a big social network site] is concerned, the bigger it becomes the more problems it has. The less it treats you with the courtesy it had when it first started. You know when you first start something you're extremely nice to everyone, you want everyone to enjoy where they're staying, you know what I mean? But when you become too big for your own good, you start treating the people who made you get there in the first place like you forgot about that. And it becomes ... no longer about the people."

– Tila Nguyen

Let's blow the bloody doors off on this one, once and for all. A social community is not a remotely new idea, nor has any particular website or business model suddenly created the notion that people *like to talk to each other*. So let's blow the bloody doors off.[107]

"It's all about people," agrees Alex Cameron. "You don't communicate with websites; this is the problem which drives me mad. It's a social anthropology question more than anything else. It's about people communicating with other people; they're not using websites. This is the thing with broadband connections: you don't buy it for the broadband connection; you buy it to look at sites. You look at a website to look at news,

177

admittedly, but effectively you're interacting with other human beings. If you read a news report, that's something that another human being has written which you are reading. And when you're on MySpace you're looking for messages from other people and sending them to other people. You're not using it cause it's a great system with great functionality, you're doing it because you're meeting new people or building an audience – and it's all based around being human."

"I'll give you a few examples of what community is," says Dave Bamforth of Faceparty.com. "We sent a message out to everyone: 'OK, we've got six million members, we've got all kinds of different jobs, so what could we do? We've got a budget of nothing, but what can we do together to try and do something?' We had a competition to come up with ideas, and the winner was 'build a school in Africa'. Basically, this is what I mean by community. We said, 'OK, who can help out with this? There must be a thousand plumbers on here, we must have twenty thousand bricklayers, and stuff.' And we got a whole school, worth £12 million, all ready to go for nothing. We had a guy offering a free helicopter; we had a guy who worked at a football factory and he blagged a few footballs; it was amazing how many people would chip in to do something. And *that* is what community is."

"And that's kind of what none of the others seem to realise: *what a community is;* but the web community is all about being *part of something.* Whereas things like

MySpace are very much like, 'Look at me!' Rather than looking at other people and helping each other out. I organised these squat parties, outside of work and I really like that. The events are put on by a whole community of people, and everyone's equal in there and everyone does their bit, no-one gets paid, but it's just for the awesome party. And that is really what community is; community isn't downloading music, that's Woolworths! There is no community at all attached to that; it's just media. A community's about people, and each other, and I think when it comes to community sites the likes of Facebook and Bebo have got the community for students and kids, whereas we're the more adult one for the 16-24 age group, and MySpace is the music one. But MySpace doesn't really work as a community, it's just loads of people on there saying, 'Look at me, look at what I can do.'"

Any more doors to blow off? Form a neat line.

Bebo And Facebook Are Knockin' At The Door Cause People Talk About Them Less

"The big threat to MySpace at the moment is Bebo. Some people are sick of MySpace. The feedback that we get from our kids is, 'I can't find what I want; I don't want a McDonalds, or Sky TV advertised at me.' You know, these things that are popping up all over the place, it's just getting a little bit silly and it's too big; you always get that kind of negative response, and it's in the news all the time, so it's not very cool. So Bebo, and Facebook, and all the others, are there – and that's what the kids are telling us." – Stuart Knight, X-Taster

"I was shocked by Bebo when I first saw it," smiles Sammy Andrews. "For kids, and for kids alone – that's kinda taken on a world of its own. But they're the next generation who are going to be conditioned this way." If Bebo does anything, it allows a younger generation to become involved with social networking on the web in a self-selected age group demographic. The underlying principles of all these sites, however, are similar indeed: music, videos, chat, connections. And maybe sales, too.

"One interesting thing that I heard," offers Ben Perreau, "is that people on MySpace were spending a lot more time on the site than they were a year ago. Everyone's saying 'MySpace is over and everyone's moving on' but I'm not sure that's necessarily true: maybe people aren't investigating it and engaging with it in quite the same way that they initially were. There's a few of them in the market now: Bebo, Facebook, Faceparty – and some of them have been around for a while and have migrated toward the MySpace model. Some of them have kind of moved away, and there are cleverer social networks that are more focused on one particular way of social networking."

"I think a year and a half ago it sat in the world of 'the fluffy, warm, internet developer,' where geeks like me would engage with MySpace because they felt it was a cool thing. The 'web scenesters' – the cool people on the web who are generally not the cool people in the real world – of which I'm probably one, have got pissed off with the fact that in the meantime so many other things have got fantastic with their technology. I guess business objectives have maybe overtaken MySpace for a bit and that's why other websites are getting the chance to edge in."

"I think it's really a cultural context of youth development," says Korda Marshall. "You know, my twelve year-old starts on Bebo, and then my fourteen-year-old goes to MySpace, and my twenty-year-old's in Second Life. Second Life's the future for me. We're doing Second Life festivals; I'm trying to break bands on Second Life. Second Life's far more exciting to me than MySpace. But in the way that eight years ago Napster was the future of music online, and now MySpace is the future, and right now it's Second Life, and then next year there'll be something else ..."

Because 'New' is 'Good', y'see. But, hey, kettles have always boiled water down the years; they might have more snazzy designs, and maybe get to the bubbling stage ever-quicker, but whack some Sild inside and it's still essentially the same ke...

Hmm, that one worked better in my head. But you know what I mean.

Second Life (And Habbo Hotel, Which Is Kinda The Same In A Load Of Ways)

It is 2006. You own a PC or a Mac, or both. You subscribe to one ISP or another and are connected to the internet. Your social networking site or web portal of choice offers online features including electronic mail, participatory message boards, news, instant messaging and all manner of people-connection chatty-chatty tools.

You can speak to people without leaving your PC or Mac.

You don't have to turn the lights on.

You don't even have to get dressed.[108]

Servers on the web network of your choice host games. One of these games is Second Life, and another is Habbo Hotel. Both Habbo Hotel and Second Life are virtual, multi-user, graphically interfaced immersion environments in which your character – your avatar – can walk around the virtual world interacting with other avatars, questing, molesting and generally being interesting. You meet each other in this virtual world and talk to each other by entering text on your keyboard.[109] And, because there are none of those restrictive multi-choice parameters that beset the traditional model of adventure games, you can therefore say anything you like. Including the same description about two web sites that are pretty mich doing the same thing.

You can have a conversation (twice in the same book). And humans like to talk (at least twice).

Second Life And Habbo Hotel therefore enable another level of communication within a virtual community that develops its own governmental and social rules dependent on the individual users and their real-world identities. They have their own economies and their monetary values have remarkably crossed from the virtual world to the real world.

Second Life And Habbo Hotel are graphical, digital social networking tools.[110]

**What All The Litigation That's Going On
At The Moment Is Really About**

Will never be expressed here. I'm not *that* stupid.

**Why Friendster May Yet Conquer The World,
Because I Promised Earlier And If I Don't Say This
Now We'll Run Out Of Book**

Friendster might yet conquer the world; their active population has steadily been rising of late due to, in part, increased and more open functionality.

But that's perhaps not the main reason why they may yet conquer the world. Nuh-uh. Here's a few facts:

On June 27, 2006, Jonathan Abrams, as inventor, and Friendster Inc., as assignee, were granted U.S. Patent Number 7069308.

This is the abstract of the successful patent, U.S., remember it, Patent Number 7069308.

Which they now own ...

... meaning this:

"A method and apparatus for calculating, displaying and acting upon relationships in a social network is described. A computer system collects descriptive data about various individuals and allows those individuals to indicate other individuals with whom they have a personal relationship. The descriptive data and the relationship data are integrated and processed to reveal the series of social relationships connecting any two individuals within a social network. The pathways connecting any two individuals can be displayed. Further, the social network itself can be displayed to any number of degrees of separation. A user of the system can determine the optimal relationship path (i.e. contact pathway) to reach desired individuals.

A communications tool allows individuals in the system to be introduced (or introduce themselves) and initiate direct communication."[111]

Got All That?

So.

Let's Try Again.

Let's *Start* Again.

Whose Space Is It Anyway?

The Meaning Of Life Explained Once And For All

Appendix One:
Endnotes/Blogs

1 Two sentences in and this is as good as it's going to get, you know.

2 This is the second best joke in the book.

3 Or not; a recent study commissioned by the U.S. government found that only 1% of Google and Microsoft's indexes produced sexually explicit pages, having filtered out nearly all the rest online. It's just what everybody looks for first.
http://www.siliconvalley.com/mld/siliconvalley/business/technology/16012389.htm – retrieved November 2006.

4 A 'book' in this sense is like a dusty, hard copy printout of an online encyclopaedia, except generally the information in it is usually written by proper people who actually base their research on tangible knowledge, rather than repeating it in a twisted and utterly superficial form from the equivalent of A Man In A Pub. A 'novel', on the other hand, is a 'book' which has a story in it that is entirely made up and NONE OF IT ACTUALLY HAPPENED. Be wary: every novel is a damned lie, and every author is a damned liar. What you are now reading is a mixture of both approaches, except less funny, less interesting and wildly less informative – but happily printed on paper that's very absorbent.

5 An archaic and somewhat odd concept – a building full of 'books' where people go to research things in those dusty, paper devices, or simply to be taken for a mug by reading them lying bastard things called 'novels'. Or,

alternatively, a place where recently-unemployed writers go to read the papers, dressed in suits, every day, to avoid having to tell their partners and families that they've been sacked for utterly unacceptable work; somewhere to ponder in the margarine silence just where exactly it's all gone wrong, and to cry silent, salt tears of frustration and distress at how the world's spinning shrug cares not for its protoplasmic flukes.

6 The irony of this is not lost on the author either.

7 My Myspace says I am, so I must be.

8 There are lies, damned lies, statistics – and wikis. This measurement is, or soon will be, a wiki. Put it online on one of those Web 2.0-style user-generated 'paedia sites, and it magically will become the accepted standard of measurement for shitness through viral repetition and rehashing. This is the world we live in, folks.

9 See forthcoming Independent Music Press book: *My Second Life* for the flipside to digital identity.

10 From time to time, however, you'll hear it claimed by archeologists that they've uncovered ancient computing devices built by, like, some Egyptian or Greek smart-arses in 42,000,000 BC. Things that look like, and are, old crappy bits of metal and/or rock with a few numbers or weird little symbols carved into them, and some encrusted vaguely moving parts that may or may not point to some stars or something. Do not listen to these people. As everyone knows, a proper and real computer is something that beeps irregularly, has cool flashing lights, spews out answers on punch cards, and wicked stuff like that. And it has to be plugged in to work, like on *Star Trek*. So ignore archeologists, because

they spend their days up to their elbows in rain-spattered farmers' fields, trawling through thousands of years of mud layers to find useless crap that previous generations have thrown away, because it was useless and crap. Archeologists are the sort of people who get rather excited when they find broken pieces of ancient pisspots in mounds of crud. That is a not entirely sane thing to spend your days doing by anybody's standards.

11 Small shiny stones and potatoes, most likely; an archaic barter system used widely before cash as we know it was invented in 1955 by Dr. Craig Cash.

12 Like in the films innit,

13 See endnote 118 in *Trivium: The Mark Of Perseverance* (Independent Music Press, September 2006) ISBN: 0955282209. Get that? What? Er, by Joe Shooman.

14 Read the section title, eh? Told you it was brief.

15 Information Processing Technology Office.

16 All hail Paul Baran: http://www.ibiblio.org/pioneers/baran.html – retrieved November 2006.

17 Which is now covered in sticky puke and rancid cider-piss from the local youths overnight, the loveable scamps.

18 The principle is this: to send information from point A to point B does not require a direct link between points A and B – a peer to peer system – but the information can take any route within the distributed – rather than centralized or decentralized – network that lies in between. It's all a bit mental and spiderwebby and stuff so I did the sensible thing and asked my homeboy Ernie about this on MSN, because he knows everything in the

world, and possibly worlds yet to be discovered, about computers. I quote, verbatim: "ok say im in china and im internetting and the route taken takes me thru the ussr but one of the main lines of the ussr goes apeshit n dies then the network can route off somewhere else to get the web page (say via india) the user doesn't notice anything just the network will be slower." Good ol' Ernie, he's boss.

19 We refer of course to the classic film offered by MGM/UA Entertainment: *Wargames*, Dir. John Badham.

20 Much in line with the athlete's problems of tennis elbow and golf ball, this is a painful injury sustained by the unguarded, accidental dropping of small mint sweets onto your naked feet.

21 This was achieved by the design and implementation of the Internet Protocol Suite in the 1970s; the Transmission Control and Internet Protocols – TCP/IP – basically are the two most important parts of Vinton Cerf's work into interoperability of networks; it is analogous with linguistics in the sense that two individuals can communicate their ideas through a common shared language, and computer programs can communicate through shared TCP/IP, therefore making the linking of very different networks possible. This is where the internet really came to life in terms of universal access.

22 In Western terms, at least. Latest statistics suggest that only 16.7% of the world's population has access to the internet, although this is growing exponentially: http://www.internetworldstats.com/stats.htm – retrieved November 14, 2006.

23 See endnote/blog 14. In a way this is a sort of
   hyperlink, ya know, in terms of internal cross-navigation
   of a document in the sense posited by Vannevar Bush in
   the Thirties and Forties in his speculative essay on the
   possible sharing of human knowledge by his searchable
   Memex system, 'As We May Think'. The concept was
   further developed by Ted Nelson in 1955, and began to
   be programmed in earnest by Douglas Englebart and
   others during the 60s. So this is a sort of hyperlink,
   albeit that it does not automatically redirect you to the
   information in question to create a trail of navigable
   information. Actually, these citations are dynamic links if
   you've a word document or a pdf copy of this book,
   which you haven't, so unless Independent Music Press
   have invented dynamic printed paper in the interim
   between the writing and reading of this book, you'll just
   have to do the linking yourself, you big computer, you.
24 Myspace.com/joeshooman
25 This online service changed its name in 1991 to
   America Online, more commonly known as AOL.
26 Alright, you don't HAVE to be naked per se, but
   titillation apparently sells books these days. Imagine I'm
   writing this in the buff, if that helps matters. I look a
   little like Leslie Grantham, apparently.
27 Whilst, quite possibly, although obviously not at all true,
   being filmed by someone somewhere, in order to
   subsequently earn a few bucks as a talking head on
   Noughties TV shows called *Weren't The '80s Fookin Boss*
   and similar, cause people DRESSED A BIT
   DIFFERENTLY, WATCHED DIFFERENT
   CARTOONS and DRUNK DIFFERENT BEER, and
   so forth.

28 See endnote/blog 14. Everything you could possibly
   want to know lives here:
   http://vlib.iue.it/history/internet/ and (albeit slightly
   out of date) http://www.davesite.com/ – retrieved
   November 2006. Indispensable here for a full overview:
   *Weaving The Web: The Original Design And Ultimate
   Destiny Of The World Wide Web* – Berners-Lee, Tim /
   Fischetti, Mark, Harper (San Fransisco), 1999 ISBN:
   0062515861

29 Bringing together existing concepts and implementing
   them with deftness, the web is still – give or take –
   based on the key programming and implementation
   concepts: Universal Resource Identifiers (URL) to look
   up web pages; Hypertext Markup Language (HTML) to
   get the net to understand what the pages are about & to
   present them in a user-friendly way; Hypertext Transfer
   Protocol to, like, get computers to talk to each other
   and fire the pages about, sorta (HTTP), all based on a
   client-server system which basically is what happens
   when your computer (client) requests information from
   a net source (hosted on a server somewhere).

30 This – i.e. my hung-over stumblings and messy slug
   through what has somehow become described as 'a
   career' – is the best joke in the book, and arguably the
   world.

31 Amazon.com was founded in 1994, initially as an online
   bookstore but quickly developed its stock into a catch-
   all, online hypershopping experience and model for
   commerce on the web. A very fine timeline of events is
   here: http://phx.corporate-ir.net/phoenix.zhtml?
   c=176060&p=irol-corporateTimeline – retrieved

November 2006. I suppose at this point it's worth mentioning *The Long Tail: Why The Future Of Business Is Selling Less Of More* – Anderson, Chris. Hyperion Books, July 2006 ISBN: 1401302378.

32 No, I don't buy it either.

33 Usually these would arrive in the same day; ladyboys had never had it so good. And I promised my mate who's currently on holiday in Thailand that I wouldn't tell anybody about his experiences over there, so don't worry DD, I definitely won't. Your secret is safe with me.

34 For a more in-depth overview of spam and statistics you'd do worse than head here: http://www.ftc.gov/spam/– retrieved November 2006.

35 This is the third best joke in the book. Are we having fun yet?

36 Previously reserved for soon-to-be-bankrupt writers of wildly unsuccessful social communication books.

37 Mostly from the people who'd written the blog in the first place, cause now they could write about how blogging was popular, and Google blogging all day before quoting each other's blogs to write new blogs about it. How very postmodern.

38 It's still there but no longer updated; Mute's current website is www.mute.com.

39 The name is from the researchers who developed the codec: Moving Picture Experts Group. For the last word on MPEG encoding in a historical context, head towards: http://www.iis.fraunhofer.de/amm/techinf/layer3 and everything will become clearer. Or, in my case, much

more confusing – even though in theory I should know all about perceptual lossy encoding and compression, because I somehow managed to squeeze a degree about this stuff out of some people who really should have known better. I honestly thought this project was going to be all about *Playboy* 'Girls Of Myspace' and things like that when I took it on. Oh well. Onward and upward.

40 Which you've nicked from Woolies, you thieving scoundrel.

41 Napster's assets were bought by Roxio in 2002 and subsequently relaunched as a subscription distribution service in 2005.

42 Christina Aguilera is now married, sadly.

43 http://www.baselinemag.com/ print_article2/0,1217,a=182560,00.asp has all the ins and outs of how all this gubbins works - retrieved November 2006.

44 Wrapped up in mysteries wrapped up in enigmas.

45 Moider (v); N. Wales general street/housing estate catch-all term meaning, variously, to 'talk nonsense'; 'to corner someone and batter their head with words'; to [rap] www.urbandictionary.net – retrieved November 2006. Wiki No.2.

46 Ludicrous, isn't it? http://news.bbc.co.uk/2/hi/uk_news/3616136.stm – retrieved November 2006.

47 This man should be knighted, truly.

48 http://www.somethingjewish.co.uk/ articles/548_jonathan_abrams.htm, July 2003 – retrieved October 2006.

49 'Making Friendsters In High Places' – Leander Kahney, *Wired Magazine* July 2003.
http://www.wired.com/news/culture/0,1284,59650,00.
html – retrieved November 2006.

50 Rumoured to have been in the region of $30 million.

51 If you were thinking about asiangrannies.com, shame on you. Insert your own joke. Literally. And no double-entendres about face parties either, please. My mum might read this.

52 Brad Greenspan's version of events is here:
http://freemyspace.com/history.htm

53 http://www.consumeraffairs.com/
news04/2006/03/myspace_inside.html – retrieved November 2006.
http://www.intermix.com/about_privacy.cfm –
retrieved November 2006
http://www.consumeraffairs.com/news04/2005/ny_spy
ware.html – retrieved November 2006.

54 On the web you can find several unscientific studies as to active accounts, but the methodology and sample groups are rather suspect. For more reliable info, on this:
http://www.webpronews.com/topnews/topnews/wpn-
60-20060224TheMySpaceMirage.html – retrieved November 2006.

55 http://www.comscore.com/press/release.asp?id=906 –
retrieved November 2006.

56 Isn't the English language great? You can make up new words all the time. I love it.

57 This is probably A Good Thing, as long as everyone involved knows the score. Previously, sex lives over the net had notoriously been a strictly one-way non-

interactive, one-in-a-bed romping experience, except with better pictures of course. Or maybe that's just me. Oh well.

58 It's obviously not his real name. I made it up. If you are really called Bob De★★★★e I apologise profusely (stifling childish laughter all the while), it's not intended to represent any part of your life in any way. But I would say this: I asked this geezer which pseudonym he wanted me to use for this and his first reply was, 'XXX10INCHESXXXUNCUTANDTHICK'. So I think we got off a little lightly.

59 Really, that's totally not his name. I don't even know what his name is, cause a mate of mine knew him and the interview was entirely conducted with said mutual friend as conduit, bashing questions back and forth through Myspace. I s'pose I'm as bad as anyone else. Again, if you really are called Eddy Z★★★★l, this isn't you. Z★★★★l is, however, my second favourite German word, after 'Knoblauch'. Oh, the fun I have in Berlin's restaurants literally never ~~starts~~ ends.

60 Eddy, I mean, not my ear. That's not all rubbery and covered in flob; though the night is young of course.

61 None of my friends though, they're all fucking weirdos.

62 For example: http://www.profilescreener.com/press.php – retrieved November 2006.

63 A lot of schools are now barring access to Myspace and other social sites; too many to list here but whack in 'School bans Myspace' into any search engine and clear a few hours to get through the pages it finds.

64 http://www.theregister.co.uk/ 2006/09/15/myspace_murder/– retrieved October 2006

65 See: http://www.bethelks.edu/collegian/
archives/002396.php – retrieved October 2006.

66 And the rules of Rugby Union. I played for Bangor
Under 15s a few times and I never had a clue what was
going on at any stage. I think I just liked tackling other
boys and punching people when the ref wasn't looking.
Until one little sod bit half my ear off in a ruck and I
retired from the sport in order to concentrate on my
drinking career. The doctor who sewed it back on was
dead fit though, so it was kinda worth it. Hey, come on,
I was 14, know what I mean?

67 I know it doesn't make much sense but it's a nice
snappy phrase innit. Wonder who I nicked it from?

68 Identity theft is one of the banes of our modern age and
Myspace is as much a victim of it as anywhere else:
http://www.9wsyr.com/news/local/story.aspx?content_
id=A0498C57-2632-40B8-8C69-E198A1D9AA2F –
retrieved September 2006.

69 http://www.dailymail.co.uk/pages/live/femail/
article.html?in_article_id=397026&in_page_id=1879 –
retrieved October 2006.

70 Totally out of this book's remit but here's the BBC
overview: http://www.bbc.co.uk/dna/
h2g2/alabaster/A676424 – retrieved September 2006.

71 The UK Home Office guidelines from the taskforce on
child protection on the internet is downloadable from:
http://police.homeoffice.gov.uk/news-and-
publications/publication/operational-
policing/moderation-document-final.pdf

72 In October, 2006, Kevin Poulsen of *Wired Magazine*
wrote some code designed to screen MySpace profiles

for convicted paedophiles, the data of which was passed onto the police. If such a concept proves workable, then this will have made the web an infinitely safer place for kids to hang out.

http://www.wired.com/news/technology/0,71948-0.html – retrieved October 2006.

73 One of the programmers on the initial Myspace project, interestingly, shared the same surname: Toan Nguyen. It's a weird world.

74 In June 2006, *Playboy* magazine, tapping into the zeitgeist as is their wont, themed their issue as 'Girls Of Myspace'; the models chosen from aspirant glamour-pusses on that site. Many other magazines have since published similarly-themed issues. So I'm told.

75 Got a problem with me writing this bit in Welsh? Oh. Okay. I'll edit it back to English later, unless I forget.

76 Not the one with the sheepskin jacket, but this version does have quite a thing for classic trainers.

77 Pitchfork's great interview with Lily Allen is here. No point me paraphrasing it; I assume as you're reading this you have an internets in your house, like:
http://www.pitchforkmedia.com/article/feature/39534/Interview_Interview_Lily_Allen – retrieved November 2006.

78 We share a (very talented) mutual friend, whose excellent music can be found at myspace.com/kayaherstad. I think I remember one particularly drunken night in LIPA's college bar when I was sat with said mutual friend; a Scottish lass came and joined us, and I think I pretty much failed miserably to engage her in a conversation which was almost

definitely about what her favourite Elvis Presley track was. Those kind of conversations always end up with me shouting at people for not picking 'Polk Salad Annie' or 'Down In The Alley'. And those kind of nights always end up with me staggering home – alone – in a foul mood, kebab falling all over my Bangor City replica shirt. Oh well.

79 As legend has it, she was signed by Craig from out of Bros. Cool or wot.

80 See endnote 118 in *Trivium: The Mark Of Perseverance* (Independent Music Press, September 2006) ISBN: 0955282209. Still by me.

81 See the not-quite-yet-forthcoming TV show, *Weren't The Nineties Fookin Boss*, presented by a whole host of other people who are apparently 'comedians' because their caption identifies them as such. This serves to imprint these people as comics within TV-land despite the evidence that a) you only ever see these people on those kind of talking head-type nostalgia clipshows, and b) they never actually say anything particularly funny. Oh, and c) I've never been asked to appear on one.

82 Plus I just thought of it and can't be arsed checking whether the notion holds any water whatsoever.

83 See, you thought all that preamble in Part One was just 'pointless waffle to get the word count up' didn't you?

84 If Web 2.0 is built on a perpetual beta concept, I don't see why books shouldn't be too.

85 Look, it's late, OK? I'm leaving it in. Call me a tosser all you like, I ain't changing it.

86 Or a Zune. Tee hee.

87 I'll translate it back into English later, unless I forget again.

88 Tony Wilson adds: "Radio One played the shit out of it for two months before it was released to download."

89 Lucy Hughes expands: "Basically there's a loserkids.com which is the U.S. version, and that was set up by Tom DeLonge and Mark Hoppus, selling clothes that they liked and they couldn't get anywhere else. That's been going for over ten years now, and then from that they started Atticus, their clothing label, and after that, Macbeth – which is the shoes [company]. Loserkids came before Atticus and Macbeth. We're the European licensees of Atticus and Macbeth and with that we also bought Loserkids UK. That's our site – we try to mirror the U.S., basically, but have a UK slant on everything."

90 Well, it's not new really; when I go and buy my ~~Lambrini~~ 90% Absinth from Windsor Wines in Toxteth, I quite often stop for a long ol' chat with main man Karl. If you ever go there, ask him about his New York story he was telling me the other week, it's boss.

91 Murdoch, not The Bear, but the twisted pun in the section title was really the best I could do I'm afraid.

92 Obviously not literally.

93 I think Mr. Wilson just earned himself a brandy to go with that planned curry.

94 Not the one out of the A-Team.

95 Although *Vice UK Magazine* editor Andy Capper responded to my question about this with one word: "Inevitable." Which is very perceptive, I think.

96 Sean also likes Absinth.

97 To be fair, there have been a number of bulletins posted

by Tom on Myspace encouraging its users to vote, and to shop responsibly, with the partnership with (RED), a percentage of whose profits go to help HIV/AIDS infected women and children in Africa. Cynical ol' Sean! Get some sleep.

98 Yeah, love the way you slipped that one in, you swine. "I was in Mexico City on a job" indeed. Pfft. I would expand on that but I've got to meet Claudia Shiffer for a drink. Of GOLD. In Monaco. On Puff Daddy's Yacht.

99 Tenner says that The Prodigy re-release 'Charly Says' sometime in the next year or so for the 20th anniversary of rave. Not.

100 Who has just earned himself a curry too.

101 Although on the other hand there's Sky+ and TiVo already, so y'know.

102 Yes, the very same. Great innit. (In November 2006 it was also announced that Myspace users – and those of other similar sites – could add the indiestore flash player to their profiles to sell music that way.)

103 Ah fair dos to ya then, Gavin.

104 Mixi.com features amazon.com recommendation-based links to potential purchases within its pages.

105 And also owns everything Metallica ever recorded.

106 Which confuses me: how did I end up with the misfits I've got?

107 Bagsy Jim Morrison, he so BUFF LOLZ

108 Alright, you don't HAVE to be naked per se, but titillation apparently sells books these days. Imagine I'm writing this in the buff if that helps matters. I look a little like Leslie Grantham, apparently. Did I mention

my short-term memory's not so good these days?

109 And, presumably, soon through VOIP [Voice Over Internet Protocol].

110 Record Companies are already hosting gigs in there; Reuters have a newsdesk there; it's insane. And it is the past and the future melded into one Matrix-type package. I can't wait to dive into it.

111 http://www.redherring.com/Article.aspx?a= 17498&hed=Friendster+Wins+Patent – retrieved November 2006. The press release can be sourced from: http://images.friendster.com/images/friendster_07_06 _06.pdf

Appendix Two:
Acknowledgements

I love MySpace. Truly, I do. I think it's great; I'm always on there and when this project came up I jumped at the opportunity to spend even more time surfing around and messing about, except this time it was 'work'. There are, no doubt, countless 'Guides To...' available elsewhere but I'm tempted to say that if you need one, you maybe shouldn't be on the site. Conversely, if you're on one of these sites already, you pretty much don't need one. So, this isn't, and was never designed as, one. Soz, la. What did, however, become very clearly obvious, very quickly, was that to try and talk about social network sites without talking about music, the web, the internet, sociology, economics, culture, linguistics, technology and blah blah blah – basically humans themselves – was a futile exercise. Music has kicked it all off, but you could equally come at it from any angle and it's as good an illustration as any. I've done my best to at least give my subjective views on a massive subject which changes every damned day. Which is of course the beauty of it all too.

And I've been able to try and do my best thanks to a host of people who gave up their time to be interviewed and/or chew the fat with me and ignore my half-arsed, dunderheaded ideas and interjections into previously very reasonable conversations.

So a thousand Linden Dollars go to Martin Roach for the support and the ridiculous deadlines (and all the frantic work on making sure this was able to happen at all, which was in rather a lot of doubt at various stages of the process for various reasons); Dave Hanley for working his balls off behind the scenes and indulging me in numerous daft late-night MSN plans; Alexandra Jackson, whose brilliant illustrations deserve many, many books of their own, which undoubtedly they will get. And thanks, by the way, Alex for making me look better than the photos.

Jon Thornton is someone to whom I owe more than I can write here without sounding like a right dingler, and though his fascinating insights, ideas, guidance and all-round genius may not have made it into the final text, they were absolutely vital in getting my remaining braincells working at all. Ernie Pollard, take a bow, you made things make sense to me too. Sammy Andrews and David Rowell both went way beyond the call of duty in helping with contacts and being so honest – and I'm going to buy them all the best curry in the world if they'll let me.

Thanks to all of the people who agreed to give up their time and offer their thoughts for input and/or interviews for the book – whether they made it to the final draft or not, I really appreciate it. So in alphabetical order, raised glasses to: Sean Adams; Dave Bamforth; Daryl Bamonte; Boypolar; Billy Bragg; John Brainlove; Alexander Cameron; Andy Capper; Jon Clark; Stuart Clarke; Peter Croxson; Dassie; Mat Flynn; Eli Fritsche; Geoff; Gavin Herlihy; Joshua Holmes; Lucy Hughes; Stuart Knight; Korda Marshall; Conor McNicholas; Joe Mott; Jamie Nelson; Tila Nguyen; Ben Perreau; Paul Rafferty; Malcolm Ramazotti; Raziq Rauf; Sam Sparrow; Huw Stephens; Martin Stiksel; Susie Stubbs; Mark Sutherland; Jen Thomas; Travis (Gym Class Heroes); Loren Williams; Anthony H. Wilson; Serena Wilson; Darrin Woodford.

And thanks also to those who were instrumental in setting things up, who did their best to set things up, or who suggested possible people to chat to and offered ideas: Jude Adams; Beth Drake; Dougie Bruce; Paul Bryan; Karen Christie; Vivienne Clore; Stuart David; Duncan Dick; Susie Ember; Siri Garber; Mike Hanson; Louise Kattenhorn; Neinke Klop; Tony Linkin; William Luff; Tim Lusher; Kas Mercer; Charli Morgan, who clearly doesn't love me anymore; Ben Myers; Dave Pichilingi; Jean Armour Polly; Gordon Ross; Elizabeth Sheahan; Nick Tesco; Sandi Thom; Karen Walter; Young Kim. Sorry if I've forgotten anyone; my short-term memory's not the best.

For general support and encouragement, which may or may not include late night whisky-fuelled plotting, poker games, transatlantic shit-talking and dodgy veggie pretend-meat-based butties: Andy Daley, Robbie Diebel, Jon Hall, Lins Kent, Roger Hill, Paul Hunt, Mike Poggione, Rob Whiteley, Karl at Windsor Wines, Woody – and all the rest of yous lot who always hammer me at Texas Hold 'Em, nice one. Though remember I'm still the only one of us to have ever drawn a straight flush, so watch out.

Special thanks to Andy Inglis.

Zoe – there are no words left.

I promised I'd mention all the Shoomans here. So: Matthew, Ann, Harry, Molly, Louis and Lily; Daniel, Louisa and Megan; Bethany and Phil; Mam & Dad, all of whom I see far less than is reasonable, hiyaaaa.

Come and see us at:
myspace.com/whosespaceisitanywaybook

Joe Shooman, December, 2006.

The best fish and chips In
the World .hmm!

Appendix Three:
Soundtrack To A Book

Starting points for surfing:
MySpace.com/voorock
MySpace.com/28costumes
MySpace.com/christinamalley
MySpace.com/1upband
MySpace.com/gofasterband

MySpace.com/ruthcullen
MySpace.com/vaffancoulo
MySpace.com/zombinaandtheskeletones
MySpace.com/apatt
MySpace.com/flamingo50
MySpace.com/connanandthemockasins
MySpace.com/kayaherstad
MySpace.com/lyonsandtigers
MySpace.com/formermissamerica
MySpace.com/maplebee
MySpace.com/jacksharp
MySpace.com/johnacousticsmith
MySpace.com/doctorspock
MySpace.com/izaboband
MySpace.com/billyenglanduk
MySpace.com/silvinightsuperstar
MySpace.com/sexeducationband
MySpace.com/bloodyhellitsthelungs
MySpace.com/fflaps
MySpace.com/skinflickx
MySpace.com/trepenna
MySpace.com/joeandthebs
Myspace.com/tilatequila

Plus a massive pile of new releases of varying quality and
the constant internal thrump and thud of the dripping
away of sanity, soul and sense. But I do love a lot of bands
including, but not limited to, Alabama 3, The Beatles, Dead
Kennedys, Iron Maiden, Irma Thomas, Rance Allen and
Motàrhead, and these people have helped me through some
very interesting times.

Appendix Three:
MyWhat? – Confessions
Of A Luddite

*"I am a Luddite. I don't do the internet and I never got MySpace.
I don't understand the need for cyber self-glorification, and I prefer
my friends to be of the flesh-and-bone variety. Things got so bad
this year someone had to sit me down and explain exactly what
the kids were doing online with MySpace and why."*

"Don't get me wrong: technology isn't bad per se.
*It changes lives. 'Americans believe, after all, that machines can do
anything: they can remove tumours, win wars, fly to the moon,'
said Wired's Jon Katz in 1995. As for me, my laptop is my life.
I sometimes wake in the night with the cold claw of fear stroking
my spine, giving me chills about what might happen if it broke
and I hadn't done a back-up."*

"But what has me scratching my head like a latter-day Stan
Laurel is technology abuse. We're suffering from an almost criminal
information overload. Consider this: The New York Times
contains more information in a single day than a person in the
17th century would be exposed to in their entire lives."

*"Technology, far from making life better, has arguably made it
worse: it's sped things up so much that satisfaction is skewed
towards instant gratification and we suffer time poverty. So
although social technologies like MySpace have the potential to be
life-affirming, we're in danger of taking the rampantly commercial,
speed-freak values that dominate the real world and putting them
into the cyber one without much thought. Sometimes MySpace
seems little more than a convenient space for kids to sell*

themselves, to turn their creativity into a marketable commodity."

Everybody wants to be somebody. No one wants to be themselves.

"Why do people put themselves online? Is it the need to make their mark? Or is it just because MySpacers want their slice of fame pie? Look at MySpace and everyone claims to be an artist, musician, writer, journalist, filmmaker, designer. Really? Everyone?"

"There's a creeping 'X-Factorisation' of culture that's spread by digital media – all those kids who think that their sole goal is to be famous and that being a singer/rock star/soul diva is easy, should you just be 'discovered' by the right producer. But creative success isn't easy. It takes years of hard graft. 'Overnight success,' said music journalist Danuta Kean recently, 'is one long night.' And technology can never be an e-passport to instant success."

Britney Vs. WMD

"Google Zeitgeist is a zippy online insight into what we spend our cyber time looking up. This annual summary of the billions of search requests made on Google turned up this depressing fact: eight of the top ten news requests of 2005 were linked to celebs or 'light entertainment'. Britney Spears was apparently far more compelling than climate change, weapons of mass destruction or the July 7 bombings."

"The irony is that we have more cheap software at our disposal than ever before. My boyfriend is a musician. Ten years ago he laboured away making electronica, spending every penny he had on horrifically expensive hardware. He eventually jacked it in, but this year got re-infected by the music bug – and found that the kit that set him back £10k ten years ago is now pretty much free, and downloadable onto any common-or-garden PC. So, we have access to the most incredible technologies but appear to be spending our time Googling Britney, plugging away on the X-Box or whoring ourselves online in the hope of hitting the big time."

The dawn of DIY media

"And yet – something's happening out there in the ether. I might not use MySpace but millions do. Bands have been broken online before they've even had a sniff at the hit parade. And traditional media is on its knees."

"Once-passive consumers are turning creators, editors and producers. Broadband is showing one of the fastest growth rates of any new technology in the UK. Specialist magazines are doing better than ever. Community radio is burgeoning. Online TV is taking off. And yes, YouTube keeps offices across the nation entertained on dull weekday afternoons."

"Even politicians are getting in on the act: in this year's U.S. mid-terms, the Democrats filmed Republicans making gaffes and posted them on YouTube. They used 'Google-bombing' to ensure that searches about Republican rivals mainly turned up embarrassing press reports, features and blogs. The Democrats' subsequent landslide victory may not be entirely unconnected to their new media dabbling."

"'This second digital wave will turn out to be far more disruptive than the first,' said the BBC's Director General Mark Thompson (somewhat ominously) earlier this year. 'It will be fundamentally disruptive, and … the foundations on which traditional media are built may be swept away entirely,' he went on, before describing his vision of a BBC dominated by user-generated content and personalised TV stations."

"So, for all technology's faults, we're on the cusp of digital media's second coming. We have the tools, and we've spent enough time on Google, YouTube and MySpace to know how to use them. And in five years' time, when the media landscape will be irrevocably different, it will have been us, the people, the MySpace users, who will have shaped it."

"Well, that's what this old Luddite hopes and dreams. Tomorrow's world is, after all, in the hands of the kids…"

Susie Stubbs
Freelance journalist, November, 2006.

Appendix Four:
A Fable From Aesop

One hot summer's day, a fox was strolling through an orchard till he came to a bunch of grapes just ripening on a vine which had been trained over a lofty branch.

"Just the thing to quench my thirst," quoth he.

Drawing back a few paces, he took a run and a jump, and just missed the bunch.

Turning round again with a 'One, Two, Three', he jumped up, but with no greater success.

Again and again he tried after the tempting morsel, but at last had to give it up, and walked away with his nose in the air, saying, "I am sure they are sour."

Appendix Five:
The Last Word Goes To...

From the transcript of the interview with Tila Tequila.

[Phone cuts out. Some Beethoven plays. Quite nice really.]

T: Heyy... my phone died.

JS: Hi! You were just about to tell me the answer to the future and everything, and the meaning of life.
[laughter]

T: Well, I mean, [I'm going to be] just extremely successful! Because I do not know what 'failure' means. With or without MySpace – regardless. I *will* achieve what I set out to do in my life. Once you've gotten this far, and worked this hard, there's just no turning back, you know?

JS: If you'd have been born ten years earlier, what would you have done? You'd have been a rock star, I think.

T: You know what, you've just gave me an idea – I'm gonna post a blog right now and ask for testimonies from fans back then and say, 'Hey guys, do you remember me on Asian Avenue? How popular I was on those sites?' So I'm gonna collect everybody's comments and that's gonna be cool to have, you know? I want to show people like, 'You know what? MySpace can't take *all* the credit for everything!' Cause these fans have followed me from back then, and I wanna show people that! Set a new light, you know?

JS: Yeah! You should do that – but you have to give my book a plug as well!

T: Oh, of *course* I will!
[laughter]

T [English accent] I'm like *this blaady waankaar from Laandannn…!!*

JS: Pretty good accent, actually! I'm in Liverpool as it happens.

T: I'm actually *drinking tea* right now.

JS: Well done! You need some biscuits to go with that. Or a teacake. And a napkin, of course. And a picture of the Queen to salute when you're drinking it.
[laughter]

JS: Well, thank you very much for talking to me. I really appreciate it.

T: Thank you very much. What's your book going to be called?

JS: It's called *Whose Space Is It Anyway?*

T: Oh, it's *definitely* mine!

I believe her, too. Go get 'em.